Thinking Sexy

Unlocking the Secrets of Sensual Desire

Amanda Lowe

Crown House Publishing Limited
www.crownhouse.co.uk

First published by
Crown House Publishing Ltd
Crown Buildings, Bancyfelin, Carmarthen, Wales, SA33 5ND, UK
www.crownhouse.co.uk

and

Crown House Publishing Company LLC
4 Berkeley Street, 1st Floor, Norwalk, CT 06850, USA
www.CHPUS.com

British Library of Cataloguing-in-Publication Data
A catalogue entry for this book is available
from the British Library.

10 Digit ISBN 1904424805
13 Digit ISBN 978-190442480-2

LCCN 2005923673

Printed and bound in the UK by
Creative Print and Design Group

For my mum
And Quentin

Acknowledgements

I would like to thank all the women who took time to answer the survey, the women who spoke to me about their thoughts about sex, and who told me that they needed to read a book like this.

Thanks also to the girls'-night-out brigade for madcap dreams and schemes and drunken evenings.

Thanks to my friends and relatives for being curious, but leaving me to get on with it.

A huge thanks and kisses to my lovely family for reminding me that there is more to life than a computer screen.

Thanks again to the Crown House Publishing team for the support and encouragement.

And last, but by no means least, a huge thank-you to editing queen Fiona Spencer Thomas for all her hard work and for patiently reminding me that my sexual fantasies might not be everyone's cup of tea, that the book will survive without a section on farting in bed, and for coming up with lots of more appropriate ways of saying 'a twelve-inch donger'.

Contents

Introduction

When I was writing this book, I got a big sheet of card and on it wrote, 'Come and talk to me about sex.' I took the card, set up a table and a few chairs in the busy city centre of Hull, got out my clipboard and went up to people saying, 'I'm doing a survey ...'

'No thanks,' they replied, as they walked away.

'It's about sex,' I added.

'Tell me more,' they would say, walking over to my table in the midday hustle and bustle to sit down and talk about sex to a complete stranger.

There's something about sex that fascinates people. I spoke to all kinds of people – young, old, sexually active, past it, not doing it yet, you name it. They all sat at my table. I spoke to men and women, but I must confess I did target women specifically. They were the ones I wanted to talk to, because this book is for women, looking at sex from a woman's point of view, so it was important to know that I wasn't alone in my thoughts and theories.

One thing they all had in common was that, as soon as they started talking about sex, thinking about sex and accessing their feelings about sex, they smiled. Every single person walked away from my table feeling happy. It had nothing to do with the table or with me: it

1

was because of their thoughts. I watched their faces grow rapturous and blissful as they spoke to me and thought about what sex meant to them. Even *thinking* about sex can change a person's internal state. It doesn't matter whether it is remembering an experience that happened years ago, fantasising or anticipating. Just *thinking* about sex can change the way you feel.

When I wrote this book I was tired of being bombarded by books, magazines and late-night television telling me that, to have good sex, I should do this, try that, buy this or look like that. Sex had somehow evolved to be all about positions, toys, endurance, experimentation and looking good. It seemed that normal people didn't have sex any more. So I went out and spoke to normal people about sex and discovered that I am normal. We normal people not only have sex, but we enjoy it, we think about it often and, no matter how good our sex lives may or may not be, we are always keen to find ways to improve.

As I didn't want to impose my thoughts and presuppositions on the people I questioned, I devised a set of questions that were very open and left plenty of room for individual interpretation. I wanted to survey all kinds of people, so the same questions had to translate across a broad cross-section of the population. Some of the interviews were conducted face to face, some via e-mail, some people were given the questions and wrote down the answers. This is what everyone started with:

THE LOWE SEX SURVEY

This questionnaire is part of the research for my current book which looks at the thoughts and the reasoning behind sex, rather than positions, toys, experience etc.

I am questioning as many people as I can, to get a wide cross section of ages, occupations, experience etc. Please forward this questionnaire on to as many people as possible – you can e-mail the answers to me and your answers will be kept anonymous.

Most of the questions are deliberately abstract – I want you to add your own meanings to the questions. There are no right or wrong answers. (Only honest and dishonest ones!)

The Questions (take as much space as you need to answer the questions and thank you for your time and your honesty)

1 *Sex is …*

2 *What does sex do for you?*

3 *Does love play a part?*

4 *What do you want from sex?*

5 *Are you a saint or a sinner?*

6 *What do you believe about sex?*

7 *What is good sex?*

8 *I want to feel …*

9 *I am …*

10 *I want …*

11 *I know …*

12 *I … sex, but …*

13 *The best time for sex is …*

14 *When I feel sexy, I …*

15 *I'm too …*

16 *I need more …*

Age

Occupation

Are you currently in a relationship?

How long have you been in/out of a relationship?

Any other comments:

Many thanks, Amanda Lowe.

What you will read in the quotes scattered throughout the book are the responses from real women of all ages and backgrounds. Talking to these women has confirmed what I had long suspected: that we don't all have, want or need sex toys, bendy bodies, multiple orgasms or even sexual intercourse in order to enjoy sex. Our most erotic organ is our mind, and that is where it all originates. We all think about sex.

This book is not a sex manual. It takes you on a journey, exploring sex in a way that I've never found in all the sex books I've read. This book is about the desire, the essence, the zest of sex and where we experience it.

It's time to taste, savour and relish the power of your most erotic organ. It's time to prime your mind for sex.

1

Clearing the Way for New Beginnings

Are you curious? Do you like to peep? If I told you that reading this book will change the way you think about sex, would you believe me, or would you have to read the whole book before you realised my outrageous claim was true? Flick through the book and have a peep, let your curiosity get the better of you, because in the following pages I am going to reveal all you need to know about sex. I'm not talking about all the positions in the *Kama Sutra* or what to do to turn your lover on. I'm talking about what goes on in your head, the thoughts you have that can turn your world around, thoughts that open the door to magical sexual ecstasy, or simply put a smile on your face on a cold, rainy day. In the course of the following chapters, I will explain how you can start 'thinking sexy', whenever you want, in any way you choose.

Sex is ...
'the passion or lust between two people'

You may ask, who am I to impart this knowledge, to discuss this holiest of holy grails? Am I really the one with the answers? How have I found these answers? Am I a sex siren who has learned the ancient art of luring men by my dazzling good looks and winning charms? Maybe I have had a long and lurid past and speak with the bitter voice of experience. Or perhaps I am a virginal nun who knows nothing of the physical act of sex but much about the spiritual aspect. Maybe I am one of those angry, ardent feminists who think that all men are bastards and that all you really need to know about sex with a man is that it's rubbish. Maybe I'm one of those older, trustworthy women, someone like your mother, your aunt, your big sister, who will tell you that all you need to know is to make sure you're on the pill and make sure he wears a condom. Well, I could be a little bit of them all, and, just so you know more about the real me, I have condensed my life into the following paragraph.

Sex is ...
'when people make love'

After leaving university, I spent several years touring Europe as The Amazing Betty, one half of Fritz & Betty's Fantastic Fire-eating Show, where I juggled, walked on stilts and ate fire. The 'rave years' in the mid-1990s were spent as a musician and were followed by the births of four children, then a decision to settle down and study how the mind works. I qualified as a clinical hypnotherapist, life coach and master of neuro-linguistic programming (NLP) and worked with clients from all walks of life. I've been having sex since 1979 and have been with my partner enjoying a healthy sex life for over twenty years. I learned most of what is in this book by talking to people – clients, friends, people like you or me – and listening to what they had to tell me.

My curiosity has always been a driving force in my life and I have written this book to satisfy my curiosity about sex. If you too are curious, maybe you'll let me be that little voice inside your mind who knows deep down that you are a wonderful, gorgeous, erotic, sublime creature. Yes, that's who I'll be as you read this book because after all, nobody knows you better than you do. You know all you need to know about sex right now but perhaps at the same time you realise that you would like to know more and that's why you are reading this book. You could be reading it to see how it measures up to what you've learned or perhaps you are simply curious. Curious is a wonderful state to be in and, although curiosity may have killed the cat, it can bring your pussy to life.

Sex is …
'loving somebody'

I want you to stop for just a moment and think about that voice in your mind – that internal dialogue you have with yourself that we all have playing most of the time. If I am going to become a temporary voice in your mind, I want it to be friendly and one you can have a laugh with that makes you feel good.

Think back to a time when you felt good, really fantastic, a time when you felt you had the world at your feet and could do anything, go anywhere and be anyone you wanted to be. The world was full of possibilities and everything was within reach. If you have never experienced a time like that or you can't remember, then just imagine how it would feel. Imagine yourself in a state of mind where you can see the potential for fun, happiness and excellence everywhere. We're just pretending here, so you can really go to town. Nobody else will even know you are doing this. They're sitting there, watching the telly, or bitching about how bad their day was, but here you are, curled up, reading this book and imagining the world is your oyster.

Visualise yourself open and receptive to new ideas. You have new ways of thinking, you are willing and able to happily cast aside all the things that have held you back and prevented you from going where you want, feeling what you want to feel and doing what you want. I'm sure I don't need to tell you this, but it feels good, doesn't it?

Let's imagine a bit more and pretend that, just for a moment, nothing else matters but the Here and Now. There's no past to worry about, no future calling you and keeping you in line, and everybody you have ever known is in temporary suspended animation, leaving you to think and act and do whatever you wish, in whatever way you want. That feels good, doesn't it? All the 'needy ones', all those people who lay claim on your mind, your time, your space, your identity, we've got them all quiet and safe, locked away, floating safely in a bubble. Nothing else matters but the Here and Now.

Sex is ...
'being close'

Let's really go to town and imagine that you have one of those stun guns that can temporarily eradicate any feelings of anger, hate, lethargy, duty, jealousy or regret. You know the sort of feelings I'm talking about here – go on, blast away, get rid of them. This is all going on inside, in your mind, so you can allow yourself to be as creative as you want. Let those feelings be little creatures that you, the superhero, are blasting away. Let rip and get rid of them.

This is simply an exercise for your mind, to get it toned up, freed from constraining thoughts and ready for anything. Go for it, zap away with that imaginary stun gun and pop anything else into imaginary suspended animation.

How good does it feel, now that you have managed to get rid of all the irritations? They are gone, either floating in a bubble or blasted with your stun gun. All your shackles are untied; there is just you and the potential to be anything you want to be. You're feeling fantastic, energised and in a state of wanton curiosity. I bet you're even smiling.

What sort of things will you be saying to yourself? What will your tone of voice sound like? Loud, soft, singsong, monotone? What does that inner voice feel like now? Where are you hearing it?

Sex is ...
'not as often as it should be'

How do you feel when you hear this voice? Where are you experiencing those feelings?

Before we go any further, we need to anchor your inner voice, those feelings and that state of curiosity. Allow yourself to really hear that voice, the feelings of freedom and unlimited potential. Anchor it.

'How do I do that?' I hear you ask.

Tell yourself that, whenever you pick up this book, you will instantly re-experience this state. Hold the book and know that each time you hold it you will be in this fantastic, amazing, curious, anything-is-possible state because you have given yourself permission to do so. Let that voice you have uncovered speak to you as you read.

Right now you are at the beginning of a journey – a journey to discover all you need to know about sex and a new way of thinking. I have the journey mapped out on the wall in front of me; you may have already travelled along a similar route but this time I'm your guide and we're here to have fun. You won't be needing passports, toys or money: all you'll need is an open mind.

By the way, any realisations, flashes of inspiration or nights of wild unbridled passion that you may experience through reading this book are all down to you – I am merely the voice in your mind.

So what happens at the beginning of a journey? Beginnings are all about energy, optimism, making room for the unexpected and the unplanned. The best beginnings happen when we can abandon any preconceived notions of what to expect. Why? So that we can experience everything from a fresh, untarnished point of view.

Do you remember the first time you learned about sex? I recall a gradual realisation that boys were different from girls and it had something to do with that thing they had between their legs. Then someone at school told me about sex – yuk! All the older kids in the playground, those worldly-wise six- and seven-year-olds confirmed that what I'd heard was the truth.

Sex is …
'good, when you can fit it in'

So I left it at that. I wasn't sure who did sex but it couldn't be any of the grown-ups I knew: they wouldn't do anything as silly as that, would they?

I dismissed sex as something that would never enter my world.

As a nine-year-old, I was forced to rethink my ideas when my mother gave me and my brother the 'facts-of-life talk' accompanied by diagrams. Is that all there is to sex? Penises, vaginas and babies?

So what was all the fuss about? Why all the secrecy, smut and innuendo?

By the time I reached secondary school, I had managed to figure out that somehow sex could be enjoyable, desirable even, but the sex-education class explained a little more to us about the subject. They told us that you don't automatically get pregnant every time you have sex. You can catch all sorts of dreadful diseases, which will make you go blind, develop nasty rashes, smell, make you infertile and can kill you. This is what having a baby looks like (turn out the lights, roll the film, catch 'em as they faint).

They tried so hard to put us off sex. And they almost succeeded. But *almost* isn't good enough. Within two or three years, we were all at it like rabbits. And why? I had heard nothing good about sex; clinical descriptions made it sound dreadful; and there were terrible, terrible consequences waiting for you once you entered the world of sex.

But I was curious about it; I no longer believed everything I heard and, admitting I knew nothing, I couldn't wait to try.

It may sound strange but our introductions to the world of sex can shape and colour how we think about sex for the rest of our lives. My intro-duction gave me a sense of curiosity, of want-ing to know more. It's like being introduced to the world of Ferraris by having someone explain the inner workings of a Ferrari engine, looking at diagrams of how it's all put together, being told the danger of

Sex is …
'good sometimes and shit others'

driving too fast and being expected to know all about driving one. It's not until you are behind the wheel, feeling the throb of the engine, smelling that leather interior and seeing the dashboard light up that the thrill of driving a real-life Ferrari hits home.

If your introduction to a Ferrari was being knocked over by one, then no amount of reading about them, having their engines explained and polishing the bonnet can take away the impression that they hurt you, they are driven by idiots and they should all be sent to the scrapyard.

The beginnings of any sexual thoughts will always contain some degree of energy because that is the essence of beginnings. Energy can be many things and the way you were introduced to sex will decide the kind of energy you experienced.

At the start we know nothing. Everything we learn, we learn through experience, we learn from others, or we decide for ourselves that it must be so.

We each paint within our minds our own individual picture of what sex is to us. First, we have a blank canvas and on it is written 'SEX'. I'm not speaking literally here: I'm speaking metaphorically. The canvas may be of one solid colour – say red, gold, black or purple – or it may be lots of different colours. We may be proud of the picture we have created and decide to hang it up for all the world to see, or maybe we paint a little picture then chop it up and burn it. But the picture we paint of what sex represents to us is inspired by what we think of sex.

Sex is ...
'intimate, connecting and a joining of souls'

The picture I paint now is very different from the picture I would have painted aged ten, fourteen or at twenty-one. That's the wonderful thing about sex: it changes and metamorphoses as we change, if we allow it to.

When you think about it, everything starts in the imagination. Each of us decides whether we want to revel in ignorance or bliss. We each decide whether we are going to be curious, angry, afraid, filled with awe or filled with pain. Unexpected, unwel- come events occur and things happen that are outside our control, but we make the ultimate decision as to how we react to any situation and how deeply we let it affect us.

Sex is ...
'definitely physical but the mind is also involved'

We began our voyage of sexual discovery drawn inexorably towards something we didn't understand. Could we have ignored those desires? Could we have altered the circumstances surrounding our introduction to the world of sex? We can't go back and change the past but we can change how we react to it now. If the picture you painted at the beginning wasn't a very nice one, stop looking at it, change the picture and start again. You don't need to carry it around with you like a talisman.

Beginnings are exciting, ambiguous and scary but it's only when we are willing to say 'I know nothing' that we are ready to learn. Beginnings are a time to wipe the slate clean, start a new canvas and paint in fresh, new colours.

Let's leap into the unknown ...

I am …
'powerful, in control'

I am …
'a bit boring'

Sex is …
'having fun with a bloke/husband/partner'

The best time for sex is …
'in an evening'

I am …
'giving, loving, loved'

I want …
'sex with him now'

What does sex do for you?
'Sometimes it makes me feel full in a very happy way; sometimes it makes it possible that I might have a child. Sometimes it makes me feel empty in a not-nice way. Always it gives me the most real sense of knowing someone. And it gives me pleasure.'

'I … love sex, but … I like to experiment'

Good sex is …
'laughing, giggling, smiling, sighing'

2

It's Not What You Do, It's the Way that You Do It

There comes a time when the unknown becomes the known. Knowing something can take on many forms. It is possible to know about sex and have a fairly broad knowledge about it without ever having experienced sex physically.

It is also possible to feel as though you know everything there is to know about sex by the very fact that you have experienced it. As with so many things in life, the more you practise, the better you are at it.

A friend of mine had a boyfriend who put a little star in his diary every time they had sex and when he reached a hundred stars he considered himself to be an expert, a master in the art of sex – and he had the stars in his diary to prove it! However, my friend confessed that stars or no stars, he still knew nothing other than a few rudimentary mechanics.

Good sex is …
'when both people have had a very tiring, fun time'

Mastering the Art of Sex involves more than reading books, watching films, talking to people or doing it lots of times. It's not a one-person show in which you are wowing your audience with your dazzling tricks. Unless, of course you are performing a one-person sex show – but that is a totally different ball game. Or is it? Essentially, having sex with someone and giving a performance are related in some way, aren't they?

I knew some people who were street performers. They juggled and did magic tricks – and very good they were, too. They had this one old standard trick in which someone lies in a long box on the ground and the other person would put these big steel blades into the box, take them out again and – *ta-daa!* Out would leap one un-chopped-up street performer to the rapturous applause of the crowd. That was the bare bones of the trick and it wasn't difficult. I had seen them do this many times and I knew exactly how it was done. I knew, as did most of the audience, that it was an illusion, but I never got tired of watching. These guys were true masters and, even though the illusion could be performed in two minutes, they never did it in less than ten, and, when they were on a roll, I've seen them make it last for twenty.

> **Good sex is ...**
> *'anything that keeps a smile on my face'*

Don't get me wrong – a twenty-minute version of what is essentially a two-minute illusion isn't necessarily an excruciatingly boring, mind-numbingly slowly performed magic trick. It can be an act of consummate professionalism. They got the audience into a state of anticipation, playfulness and curiosity, made sure they were all there with them, enjoying the ride, going along with the spirit of it all and entering into their world. It wasn't until they knew that they had them captive, hanging on their every word that they even started the magic trick. All the time, they were joking about, quipping, bantering with the audience and each other, never once missing a beat, yet making the audience feel involved and doing it all effortlessly. The thing was, the illusion itself was easy. The skill was keeping the audience interested, making it worth their while to stand and watch and making sure that, when they went on their merry way afterwards, they felt good. This whole rapport-building thing was made to look effortless, while they misdirected the audience into thinking that it was difficult and deadly dangerous.

I once saw the same illusion performed by a different pair of street entertainers who got the guy into the box, shoved the blades in, took the blades out, got the guy out of the box and that was it. *Ta-daa!* Exactly the same illusion, but this time the two-minute trick was performed without love or finesse in about a minute and a half.

They had no communication with the audience – it was as though they had a trick to perform and they were going to get it over and done with as quickly as possible. That's not what performing is about. It's a two-way communication between the performer and the audience. A good performer

Good sex is …
'anal sex; dirty sex; hand jobs!'

watches the audience taking their cues from them and silently says to them, 'Stay with me for a while and we'll enter another world. I'm here and I'm ready – let down your defences and I'll bring you into my world. We can suspend disbelief for a while and let the magic happen.'

I'm not just talking about street entertainers here. Think about all the performers, entertainers, singers, writers, filmmakers, comedians, sports people and even lovers who make a positive impact on you, who move you in some way. You allow yourself to enter their world and enjoy what you find there and maybe even return for more. Even though you may hear the same song a hundred times, you never tire of it. There has been a two-way communication and the magic has been allowed to happen.

I knew another entertainer who travelled the world with his act, the props for which consisted of a bag of pegs – those good old-fashioned wooden-with-springy-bits clothes pegs. I can't remember what he called himself – The Great Peggo, or something like that. He presented himself as a strongman and then proceeded to spend the next half-hour putting pegs on his head and fingers. He was German and would engage the audience with High Medieval Gothic dialogue, and, although I never understood a word he said, I loved the way he spoke, the way he performed and the fact that he could whip up an audience into a state of frenzy at the climax of his act by putting a peg on his tongue. It wasn't the peg going on to the tongue that whipped them up, but the way he did it.

> **Good sex is ...**
> *'when you try to please your partner and they try to please you'*

Communication is more than the words we say. I could understand what The Great Peggo was communicating, even though I didn't understand a word of it.

Mastery comes into place the moment we realise that communication is never a one-sided affair: it requires give and take.

What about the relationship between lovers? When I talk about 'mastery', I am not talking about 'power over', 'dominance' or the word 'master' from a male perspective. For me mastery, in terms of sex, is not a description of conquest, victory, command or superiority. It is more to do with skill, dexterity, proficiency and ability to make the magic happen. The reverse of mastery is the qualities that make for a not-so-hot lover – timidity, shyness, self-deprecation, poor self-image, poor self-expression, weak will or lack of imagination. In itself there is nothing fundamentally wrong with being timid or shy. In the right place and at the right time, timidity and shyness can be a positive turn-on, but when they get in the way of communication they can severely interrupt the flow of good sex.

Learning the art of mastery in sex is all about being aware of the unlimited possibilities available, opening ourselves up to promising ideas and being willing to take the initiative occasionally. It is about learning a craft, a skill, an art, and using it to exert a positive influence over another. Here is a simple fact: once you learn to love sex, to enjoy it, to play with it, there is no end to the fun you can have. Once you glimpse the potential that awaits you in terms of pure hedonistic pleasure, if nothing else, then mastery of sex is this season's must-have major accessory.

Think of the upsurge of energy and exciting new openings awaiting you. Start imagining all the opportunities there will be to delve into the unexplored. You have learned your trade but are not fully adept at it – yet. You have within you all the potential skills and creative abilities that you will ever need – it's just that some of them may be hiding. Don't worry about that: they'll manifest the moment you are ready, and that is what this book is all about. Soon you will be manifesting

Good sex is …
'lust, desire and mutual understanding'

those all-important skills and creative abilities that will turn you into your own personal sex magician.

So where does this magic, this ability to have this spellbinding sex, come from? Well, I'll tell you where it *doesn't* come from. Let's get some of those myths out of the way for a start.

Myth 1:
Spellbinding sex doesn't come from knowledge

Yes and no. Knowledge can help but it doesn't make the magic.

Imagine that I found a university that was giving out degrees in sex (there probably is one somewhere) and I enrolled on the course. Imagine that I spent the next three or four years learning everything there was to know about sex that was written in books, films and magazines. If I wrote papers on surveys about sex, would it make me better at it? I would probably discover a few interesting techniques and ideas along the way and I would know all the tricks that would make a good performance, but would all this knowledge guarantee the magic? I don't think so.

Good sex is ...
'being ragged all over!'

Myth 2:
Experience doesn't make us better at sex

A hundred little stars in a diary won't necessarily make you a better lover. Nor will having a hundred lovers or knowing a hundred different positions. Experience in itself is not a passport to magical sex.

But surely it can stack up the odds a bit, can't it? Sooner or later, if I have enough sex, with enough different people, in enough different ways, I'll strike lucky, won't I?

> **Good sex is …**
> *'where the orgasms are nonstop'*

Not if you don't learn from your experience.

Knowledge on its own won't necessarily hit the spot and experience alone won't hit the spot either. Think back to a time when you were having sex and it was amazing, magical, fantastic, or simply hot and heaving and everything you needed right at that moment. Or that quickie you had that lasted only a minute but put a spring in your step all day. When you were there, experiencing it in the moment, you wouldn't consciously have been comparing it with other times. Nor would you have planned and structured your movements. Maybe before or afterwards but not right there and then, when you were in the throes of passion. When the sex is good enough to lose yourself in – even if it's only for a few seconds – the last thing you think about is knowledge or experience. Which brings me to the next myth.

Myth 3:
The longer the sex lasts, the better it is

People in the movies get to have sex that lasts all night. Not only that, they do it through a soft-focus lens with a sexy soundtrack-playing away in the background. They manage a few moments of sleep as dawn approaches and then they have one more round of lovin', leap out of bed, hit the shower and are ready to save the world in ten minutes flat.

Good sex is ...
'adventurous sex'

We all have fantasy ideas of amazing sex sessions, but real life changes things.

Some people believe that the only good sex is the sort that goes on and on and involves multiple orgasms. Others have told me that the only good sex is the bad sex – the rough, raw and dirty sex. Over time we begin to realise that good sex is not about the sex: it's about what is wanted at that particular time.

These needs and wants can change from moment to moment, from partner to partner, even on your own. Being aware of the wants and needs of anyone involved can make the magic begin.

3

The Inner You

Being knowledgeable about sex, having lots of experience, the length of time you take or the number of orgasms you have, will not automatically guarantee a consistently good sexual experience. Whether a particular sexual encounter is good or not and even whether sex itself is good or not is open to personal interpretation. Judging something to be good or not good is purely subjective and its value relies on individual interpretation and context. Imagine if I'd stopped writing for a few minutes, nipped out, had sex and was now sitting here telling you all about it. I might say, 'That was the worst sex I've ever had in my life: there was no attempt at foreplay and it was over before it had hardly begun.'

Or I might say of the same experience, 'That was bloody fantastic – I haven't had sex for months and that was exactly what I needed.'

What does sex do for you?
'Makes me smile'

It all depends on the context – the context can change how we value something and how we interpret our reactions to the situation or experience.

Knowledge, experience, time and numbers are all measurable, all quantifiable.

I can ask,

- 'How many different positions do you know?'

- 'How many times a week do you have sex?'

- 'How long on average does your sex last for?'

- 'Do you have orgasms? Sometimes? Every time?'

No matter what you told me, I still wouldn't know whether you had a satisfying sex life.

I could tell you what I get up to and you could have a go at doing it my way but that wouldn't guarantee that the magic would happen for you. You could give me step-by-step instructions on how you hit the jackpot every time – I could follow your directions and end up with nothing.

What does sex do for you?
'Fills the gaps between TV and shopping'

So how come all this measurable, quantifiable experience that can be broken down into step-by-step instructions doesn't automatically translate into good sex?

Because it's only surface knowledge. None of it makes any allowance for what goes on inside our heads; and what goes on inside our heads – your head, my head or anyone else's – is not measurable or quantifiable. One can't measure intuition, mystery, secrets or imagination. Besides, it's nobody else's business what goes on in your head.

Why shouldn't this be a shared process, in which everyone gets involved?

**What does sex
do for you?**
'The ultimate high'

Well, we can invite anyone we like to our party. We can dance till dawn, whoop it up all night long, toss our heads back, throw our arms in the air and laugh, laugh, laugh – but the only one who truly knows whether you're having fun or faking it is you.

You are the one who has the last word on how much you are going to enjoy something. You are in control of your reactions and your feelings. If there is someone with you who is determined that you will have a good time and you are equally as determined that you are not going to have fun, guess who wins. If you decide that you are going to love something, no matter what – and all kinds of situations spring up to test your resolve – the ultimate decision as to whether or not you continue to love it is yours.

Let's explore and probe a little deeper to see what lies below the surface knowledge and beneath the version of ourselves that we present to the world. You and I both know that who we are on the surface is a very different person from the person who lies, untamed and unchecked, deep inside.

But what has this 'inner me' got to do with sex?

Everything.

I can't physically caress my mind. My mind doesn't orgasm. How then, can what goes on in my mind affect how I feel sexually?

Let's play for a moment. This is something you can try, wherever you are, to illustrate how powerful your mind is when it comes to feeling sexy.

Make yourself comfortable and, for a moment, stop and think about a time when you felt sexy, horny, hot for it, hungry, ready for sex, passionate, when your juices were flowing and, if you didn't get what you wanted soon, you felt you might explode.

Don't do it yet – start in a moment. You may find it useful to close your eyes and fully immerse yourself in the feeling, so read through to the end of the paragraph before you start letting your mind loose. As you dip into that feeling, let yourself flow with those sexy, horny, hot-for-it, hungry, ready-for-sex sensations. Increase the feelings and, as they reach a peak (within thirty seconds or so), take in a deep breath, a slow, languorous, deep breath, hold it for a second or two and then blow the breath out, gently through your lips. Have a quick skim over the paragraph so that you fully understand what to do, then go for it.

What does sex do for you?
'Makes the relationship that bit more exciting'

Now, imagine you are the sexiest beast alive. We're delving into your mind, playing with the inner you here, so be as playful as you want. Nobody else will ever know. If you were the sexiest beast alive – and you are, you know – how would you move? What would you sound like? What would you look like? Take a moment or two to build up this picture in your mind – you are the sexiest beast in the world – and make it as tempting and compelling as possible. When you have created that image of yourself in your mind, turn up the feelings, change the colours to make it hotter, bring it closer, brighter, and make it more focused. Enjoy yourself and see what you would see, hear what you would hear, say what you would say and feel what you would feel.

Let all those sights, sounds, images and feelings loose in your mind; increase the feelings and, as they reach a peak (within thirty seconds or so), again take in a slow, languorous, deep breath, hold it for a second or two and then blow the breath out, gently through your lips. Have a quick reread of the last paragraph and try it for yourself.

Are you still having fun? Fantastic!

What does sex do for you?

'Definitely makes me feel closer to hubby and makes me feel feminine'

One last thing to play with: when you've read the next paragraph, close your eyes and experience this as fully as you can.

Imagine yourself on the brink of orgasm, ready to explode. If you've never experienced an orgasm, imagine how you would like it to feel. You don't actually have to be on the brink of or to experience a real orgasm: just imagine it. Open up to that inner part of your mind, have fun and play for a while. Remember when you were little and played at being a witch or a fairy, or a nurse, or a pony? You knew you weren't a real witch or fairy but you just pretended, acted 'as if' and had fun. Close your eyes and pretend you are on the brink of orgasm. Let that feeling well up and grow inside you; let your mind's eye see what it needs to see, hear what it needs to hear, feel what it needs to feel, say what it needs to say to take you mentally to the brink of orgasm. Let it intensify and build and, as this orgasmic feeling reaches its peak, let all those sights, sounds, images loose in your mind. Increase the feelings and repeat the breath technique.

You've just experienced three examples of the power of your most erotic organ – your mind. You haven't needed to do anything other than imagine, and you were there, experiencing those feelings almost as intensely as you would in the physical world.

What you also did just now was to anchor those states to the breath. Remember that slow, languorous deep breath you took as the feelings peaked? That was anchoring those feelings, and we'll be testing that anchor before the end of this chapter. We use anchors all the time, most of the time without even realising. When you hear a song on the radio and it takes you back to that crazy, carefree time when you first heard it – that's anchoring. When somebody says your name in a certain way and you feel like a little girl again – that's the anchoring process working. Scents are powerful anchors: the smell of sandalwood always takes me back to being in India; Estée Lauder's Youth Dew perfume always reminds me of my mother. Our minds associate intense feelings and memories with certain anchors, conditioning our feelings and reactions without our even realising.

The awakening of senses, perceptions and ideas begins in the mind. The mind also holds our false feelings, pretence and patterns of emotion. Sometimes it holds them so well that what is really there – our natural sense of curiosity, genuine responses and unbridled emotions – could be hidden deep down, under layers of conditioned feelings, patterns of behaviour and self-imposed imperatives.

What does sex do for you?
'Everything – when it happens!'

As we begin to probe a little deeper, delving below the side of ourselves that we present to the world, we start to discover the important part that lies untamed and unchecked. This can be liberating and it can also be scary. Should we open up the Pandora's box and let loose that undeveloped potential and the darker sides of our personality? Perhaps we will discover some hidden pattern at work in our sex lives.

That's the beauty of the mind. It doesn't deal in absolutes. Physically, someone is either touching you, or not. They are lying on the bed, or they're not. A person is having sex with you or they aren't having sex with you.

The mind doesn't deal with things that are either black or white: it constantly moderates and the context is the moderator.

Take a moment, sit back, close your eyes and take in a deep breath, that slow, languorous, deep breath, hold it for a second or two and then blow the breath out, gently through your lips. Do it now. Go on, don't try to work out why, just do it.

There. Did you get the hit? Did the anchor work?

What does sex do for you?
'Stirs me at a really primal level'

You didn't have sex in the physical sense just now but your mind allowed the anchor to recreate those feelings. You couldn't rationalise it by saying, 'That was sex – I always feel like that after sex' because it wasn't sex in the physical sense, was it? The mind doesn't deal in absolutes, it works with contexts. You gave yourself a powerful anchor and your mind obliged.

We'll get back to the issue of black and white and absolutes later on in this book but for now, enjoy being a bit playful.

When I was a little girl and played 'pretend', I liked to have all the trimmings and trappings of my chosen character. If I was a witch, I would have the hat and the mad laugh. When I was a fairy I needed wings and a wand and I couldn't be a nurse without wearing my cape and the apron with a red cross.

However, when I was drifting off to sleep at night, I could be whoever or whatever I wanted without the costume, because I had them all there in my mind. I had everything I needed to be whatever I wanted inside and I still do. So do you.

I know that counting how often you have sex won't necessarily improve your sex life but being aware of your own personal abundance, although it sounds similar, is an altogether different story.

What does sex do for you?
'It makes me feel happy, safe, loved, sexy and, most importantly, satisfied'

4

Personal Sexual Abundance

Being aware of your own personal abundance? What's that all about? And what exactly is meant by 'abundance'?

Personal abundance is about having a sense of plenty, profusion, richness, wealth, flow, exuberance and bountifulness. Once we become aware of our own personal sexual abundance, we open ourselves to thinking about possibilities.

I'm not talking about sleeping around and being promiscuous. That is what we might call an abundance of sex but it isn't necessarily personal sexual abundance.

Personal sexual abundance is about experiencing a feeling of fertility – a fertile mind, fertile imagination, planting seeds of possibility and watching them grow.

The opposite of personal sexual abundance is personal sexual scarcity. This manifests itself whenever we focus on what we consider to be a problem.

The best time for sex is … *'on the spur of the moment'*

It's like being director of a stage full of performers, props, scenery, clever lighting, special effects – the whole caboodle is up there at your disposal. For whatever reason, you as the director choose to shine a harsh spotlight on one sad little character. Nobody else, including you, can see any of the stars on the stage, waiting to do their bit, because all the focus is on that one insignificant person. Until you change the focus, that is all anyone will see.

The best time for sex is …
'whenever you feel like it'

Every year, my secondary school put on a school performance. The director would always choose productions that allowed for as many bodies on stage as possible. Inexplicably, every scene would have fifty or sixty little Mexicans, angels, Egyptian slaves or pirates, sitting or standing somewhere on the stage.

'There is method in my apparent madness,' the director would say to her critics. 'Fifty or sixty kids floating around on stage will bring fifty or sixty families to watch the production. If they're in every scene, then the audience will never get bored, because there will always be something interesting to focus on. Even if the production stinks, which it won't, there will be something in it for everyone.'

Along a similar theme, my most successful mealtimes happen when I slap a selection of all kinds of food on the table: ham, cheese, eggs, salad, jam, honey, fruit, beans, bread, bagels, in fact whatever I can pull out of the cupboard. I know it sounds like a very bad meal, but to my kids and whoever else happens to be sitting at the table, it is utter magnificence. They can each have exactly what they want; everyone is happy, well fed. And all I've done is opened up a couple of cupboards and a fridge. Personal sexual abundance will give you choices, control and that great feeling of being able to give *without effort*. Sexual stinginess, the flipside of the coin, offers very little in the way of choices and makes it difficult to give freely.

You might ask, 'What am I supposed to be giving?' Anything you want. What can you give? What do you need or want to give? How about 'time' for starters? If you want to give yourself time to enjoy sex and you haven't got any time to give, what do you do?

Whenever I find myself in that situation, I have two choices:

- I tell myself that I haven't got time to enjoy sex and resign myself to not enjoying sex or having no sex at all; or

The best time for sex is ...
'any time and any place'

- I make time to enjoy sex, which is by far the most satisfying solution, and, with the help of personal sexual abundance, it isn't a difficult choice.

Be warned, though: 'abundance' is a strange word. It means 'lots of', 'plenty', 'overflow', and personal sexual abundance is lots of, it's plentiful and it's overflowing with whatever we put our focus on. Charge up your personal sexual abundance and you will have an abundance of whatever you pick. If you focus on how bad your sex life is, that's what your personal sexual abundance will give you – by the cartload. If you focus on how wonderful your life is becoming, that's what your personal sexual abundance will provide. It's a strange phenomenon but even if occasionally you get thrown off course by all those little trials and tribulations that life hurls at you to make sure you are still alive, your focus will get you back on track. Or it might keep you off the track, depending on where your focus lies. It can be as wide or as narrow as you like. The wider your focus, the more choices you give yourself, but then you may not necessarily want a lot of choices.

When consciously you choose what to focus on or what you want an abundance of, you give yourself the power to turn around your sex life. What you choose will determine the way it is turned around.

If you're still not convinced, try this little experiment. The next time you are in the mood for sex, focus your attention on whether your bottom's too big, or too small, or worry about whether your feet smell. Try focusing on the fact that you might be getting a headache. See how passionate, how spontaneous, how fulfilled, how sexy that makes you feel. We've all done it.

Trying to enjoy a night of passion with a mind swamped with worries and niggles is just about impossible. It's amazing how active your mind can be once it starts on the 'bitching about self' track or the 'I've got so much to do' line of thought. Tell me that you too have had sex wondering how quickly you can get this over and done with because you have things to do. Tell me that there hasn't been a time while you've been in the throes of passion, making all the right moves and all the right noises, and your mind has been wondering what colour to tile the kitchen.

The best time for sex is ...
'night-time when the kids are asleep'

We've all been there, wallowing in our personal sexual abundance. So what did we get an abundance of?

The second part of this experiment requires you to focus on how wonderful you and your partner are and what a fabulous body you have. Concentrate on the incredible feelings you are having, how good you are feeling and how sexy you feel. Focus on the wild, hedonistic pleasure-seeker who is about to burst out into the world.

You can concentrate your personal sexual abundance thoughts on whatever you like, but make sure they are positive thoughts. No griping or moaning this time – unless, of course, they are moans of pleasure.

The best time for sex is … *'when the kids are out at rugby'*

Imagine you were sitting down for that chaotic but plentiful feast in my house and focusing on the jar of chocolate spread on the table in front of you. Imagine you hated chocolate spread and spent the entire meal staring at it thinking: 'I hate chocolate spread – what a rubbish meal I'm going to have! There's chocolate spread on the table and I hate the stuff.'

To be sure, you would have a bad experience of eating *chez moi*.

However, if you looked at the table and saw all the other foods heaped on it and heard me say that, if there was anything you fancied eating that wasn't there, holler and I'd find some, then you would be able to eat something, probably enjoy it and not worry that it wasn't the same as what everyone else was eating. You might even notice that everyone was eating wildly different things that they had each selected and everyone was happy.

We get what we focus on – well, not necessarily *get* what we focus on, but we certainly attract more of the same. So what do we want to focus on?

The best time for sex is …
'when I'm on holiday and can have more time'

This may sound obvious, but I'm not you. I haven't lived your life; I don't know the people you know; I don't have the same thoughts as you. So I can't tell you what to think. I can't tell you that, if you do this or do that, your sex life will automatically improve. I can't tell you things to do that will have your lover begging for more and guarantee more orgasms than you've had hot dinners. I've read those books that offer instant pathways to pleasure if you do it this way or that way, and I don't know about you but they rarely work for me. The tips, techniques and positions may well suit the authors and they can inspire the reader to do or try different experiences, but they cannot guarantee that everyone will get the same results, because we have all had different experiences in life.

I am not here to tell you how to think or what to think because I haven't lived your life and I have no idea how you think. I don't know what turns you on; I don't know how you like to have sex or even if you have sex at all. All I am offering you in this book are ways to look at things differently and ideas to open your mind some more and embrace possibility thinking. I am sowing the seeds of ideas and it is up to you to fill in your day-to-day details and decisions. It's up to you to decide whether you want to water those seeds and watch them grow.

If you have never realised that your sexuality is something valuable and precious, an important part of nature and one of the pleasures of daily existence and reading this book makes you more aware, fantastic. I'm not telling you anything you didn't already know, merely making you aware of things that you may not have realised you knew. Your personal sexual abundance begins and ends with you. Nobody else can bestow it on you or impose it on you. Nobody else can tell you the best way to experience your personal sexual abundance. Well, they can tell you all they like, but you have the ultimate decision as to whether you take a blind bit of notice of what anybody else thinks.

Look at all that latent sexuality floating around out there. It's all yours, every last bit of it. Take as much sexual abundance as you want. There is enough for everyone – claim it, own it, and, once you accept ownership and control of your personal sexual abundance, that is the moment you become powerful.

> **The best time for sex is …**
> *'the morning – as long as both of us have brushed our teeth'*

I am …
'very happy with my sex life'

What does sex do for you?
'Wears me out'

Good sex is …
'money for a kebab and the taxi home'

Sex is …
'beautiful'

'I … *love* **sex, but** … *so does everyone I know'*

I need more …
'free afternoons'

I want …
'to feel good'

I am …
'not as confident as I want to be'

Sex is …
'something that is really great once you get into it; it's a fun, naughty and dirty part of your relationship'

'The actual sex act is way out of proportion to the hundreds of column inches written about it each year and the emphasis put on it by press, advertising and religion – but it sells, salacious gossip in particular sells and everyone can be hypocritical about it.'

I want …
'to be happy'

Sex is …
'fantastic sometimes'

5

Sex and Power

So, what has power got to do with sex? Everything. Never underestimate power when it relates to sex.

However, the concept of power does not always sit comfortably with us females. Sometimes we crave it, feeling as though we have none, and sometimes we are scared of it, afraid of the responsibilities that come with it. Power, like abundance, is a double-edged sword. It has negative connotations surrounding expressions such as 'power over', 'power-crazy' or meanings such as 'overpowering', 'forceful', 'dominating' and 'commanding'. It also has positive meanings and associations: 'identity', 'authority', 'leadership', 'self-control', 'experience', 'knowledge', 'potency', 'ability', 'talent'. Not only that, the negative and positive sides are interchangeable depending on their context.

> I am ...
> *'sex personified'*

Do you remember when you were a teenager, rebelling against people in power? Those people could be absolutely anyone: parents, teachers or anybody we thought had power over us. And what did our little rebellions give us? That's right – power. It wasn't always that 'Nah na-ne nah na: I've won – you've lost' power we wanted. It was

41

the power of knowing where our personal boundaries were and how far we were willing to push them. It was the power that comes from knowing we didn't automatically have to do what people told us, the power that comes from realising that there's more than one way to do something and the way you've been taught isn't necessarily right for you.

Teenage rebellion comes from a dawning awareness of power. We all have that power within ourselves – the power to say yes, to say no, to make our own decisions and make ourselves heard; but this power lies dormant within us and most of the time we don't even realise it's there.

After the teenage rebellion phase dies down, most of us get back to conformity. Sometimes we assume that conformity is the stripping away of power, that in order to conform with what society expects of us we must give up our personal power. That's the wonderful thing about power: it's with you always. You bestow upon yourself the power to conform and maintain that conformity. You give yourself the power to be a nonconformist. You take your power and decide that you couldn't give a hoot about whether you are conforming or not – you are going to do your own thing.

> **I am ...**
> *'sexy – a sex goddess at times!'*

Personal sexual power is about choice. It is about being aware that we have choices and it is we who make the decisions. If you decide for example that you have gone off sex or don't want to have sex for whatever reason, then you have chosen to exercise your own personal sexual power. Power works both ways: it can be positive or destructive, depending on the context.

You might, for example, decide to abstain from sex to annoy a partner, for religious reasons or for health or social reasons. It's the same decision but with different contexts, different meanings and different interpretations.

Feeling powerless sexually, can be a result of many things. Don't get me wrong here – feeling powerless sexually isn't necessarily a negative thing. It can be a huge turn-on. But, again, it all boils down to context and situation. If I am naked, blindfolded and tied to a chair, I would probably enjoy that feeling of powerlessness if it was my partner who was playing with me. If it was some crazy sex fiend, even if they did exactly the same things my partner did to me, I wouldn't enjoy my powerlessness. That is the assumption – but who knows? I might hate it with my partner and have the time of my life with the fiend. That's the thing with personal sexual power. There are no absolutes. You set your own rules and change your rules as often as you want.

I am …
'cautious'

Maybe you dislike authority, have no self-control, there's a lack of ambition, you feel immature, or perhaps you see those qualities in someone else. Now, do you see those qualities as positive or negative?

Allow me to let you into a little secret. It really doesn't matter how you interpret power or lack of power. What really matters is how you see and react to your perception and how it affects you.

We each have our own little hierarchy of what is important to us, what turns us on and what we find acceptable. We can list these preferences in order of importance and the things that are the most important to us will be the things that we give the most power to.

I am ...
'not ready yet'

We can categorise anything we want and build our personal hierarchies in any way we want. If we build our own order of personal preferences, why should we nominate, arrange and give power to things that give us a hard time and make our lives miserable? Why do we so often choose to disempower ourselves by giving power to thoughts, ideas, situations that we don't want?

Once I had a subconscious list of what I wanted from sex and somewhere high up on that list was 'not to wake the children up'. If you don't have children, you may think this a strange thing to appear on a 'what I want from sex' list, but, if you have kids, you'll know exactly why it was important to me. It's probably on your list as well. As this priority became more and more important, it began to cancel out my first two wishes, which were 'closeness' and 'relaxation'. We would end up getting close, relaxing and then going to sleep. Where's the problem, then? My top three 'what I wanted from sex' criteria were satisfied – but *I* wasn't satisfied. No sex at all wasn't what I wanted, even though in a perverse way it fulfilled the criteria.

Don't worry: all was not lost. Like most couples who like sex and who also happen to have children, I found a way to have my cake and eat it.

I reconsidered what I wanted from sex. I realised that I can get closeness and relaxation without having sex and that the children will or won't sleep, irrespective of whether I am having sex. I also realised that I was giving these three things too much power. So what did I change? What else did I want from sex?

I wanted to feel rude and wild, to experiment and play. I also wanted to feel closeness and relaxation and not to wake the kids up, but not as much as I wanted the fun ideas. So I put them higher on my list, decided they were more important to me than the first list, and gave them more power.

It's amazing, but, once you consciously give power or authority to something, your mind works hard to make sure that you get it. Sex is one of the forces that drive your mind. So, irrespective of whether it is positive or negative, if you give power to certain situations, thoughts or feelings about sex, your mind will work hard to make sure that these manifest themselves.

I am ...
'up for it'

What do *you* want from sex? Let's get a little more specific: what do you want from sex that you aren't getting now?

Think of what sex gives you at the moment and mentally replace the top three things with the most important three that you want but aren't getting at the moment. Next time you're on a promise, give some power to those three new important wants and see what happens.

When you give power and importance to what you want from sex, you can make it as desirable, enticing and sensual as you wish. It doesn't have to be practical. You will begin to see the effects of the potency of these new values almost straightaway.

That's another wonderful thing that happens when you set your own rules about your desires: you have the power to change them whenever you want. You are in charge, you call your shots, you have absolute power over how you want to feel at any given moment. All you have to do is claim it.

Powerful people are very often ambitious people. Have you ever thought about what ambitions you have about sex? I'm not talking about sexual fantasies here – more about that in a later chapter. Is there anything you would like to achieve sexually that you haven't yet achieved? Maybe you are one of those lucky people who have done everything they want to sexually. How wonderful it must be to have dreams, ambitions, plans and to achieve them all. There is after all only one thing that can prevent us from fulfilling our sexual dreams. Ourselves. We give ourselves power; we feed the fire of our ambitions; we have the dreams; we are the one who can make or break the power.

I am ...
'a nymphomaniac'

If I can decide exactly what I want, who I want to be and how to feel, shouldn't I have some kind of personal sexual philosophy on which to hang it all, something that makes sense to me, something that drives me either to fulfil my sexual ambitions or blow them out? What if my dreams and schemes lead me in a direction I'm not happy or comfortable with, or have a negative effect on others? How do I test the water to find out if it's what I really want?

Now we are seeking answers to the enigma that is our sexual self. Our sexual self is how we express our personal sexual philosophy.

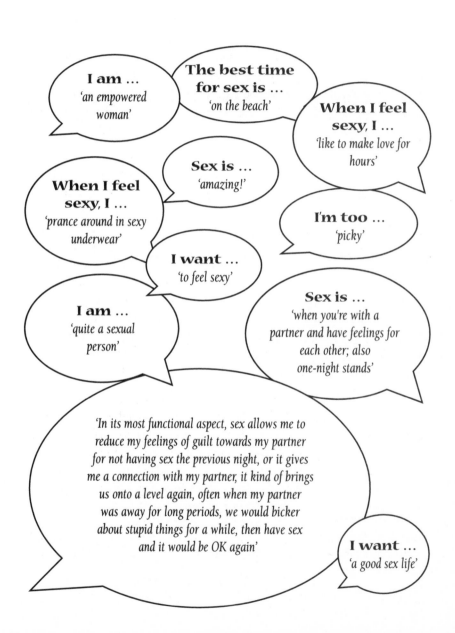

6

Personal Sexual Philosophy

In order to use and express our personal sexual philosophy, we have first to know what it is. Each of us has his or her own and, like our fingerprints, each is unique but, unlike fingerprints, philosophy can be changed.

So, what is a personal sexual philosophy? A personal sexual philosophy is a set of guidelines we set ourselves to determine how we react and respond to sex. These can be adopted from anywhere, imposed on us by anyone or anything, or made up by ourselves. Our personal sexual philosophies are created from our beliefs and values about sex and ourselves. We have picked them up, often subconsciously, throughout our lives.

Beliefs and values don't mean the same thing but they are related to each other. The things we value, whether good or bad, are the things to which we subconsciously give power. Beliefs are the personal rules we give ourselves about what we can or can't do, what we find acceptable, what turns us on and off. Often we don't even realise that we have certain beliefs and values and can surprise ourselves when those that have lain dormant occasionally surface.

Are you a saint or a sinner?
'Definitely a sinner'

To uncover your beliefs and values about sex, ask yourself:

- 'What is important to me about sex?'

- 'What is important about my sexuality?'

Then complete the following statements:

- Sex is ...

- Sexuality is ...

Don't just give one answer to each question or statement. Keep on going until you have at least ten definitions, then give yourself ten more. When I'm working with a group of people and I ask them to answer these questions and statements, no two people ever come up with the same answers. Try it next time you're out with your friends. Try it with your lover. You will soon realise why there is no such thing as a standard, one-size-fits-all sexual philosophy.

We have all lived different lives, have different beliefs and values, and our sexual philosophies are as individual as we are. They are moulded by many different things and can change in an instant or be held onto for a lifetime.

For most of us, our personal sexual philosophies are a closely guarded secret. This isn't a bad thing in itself, except that we tend to hide them even from ourselves. Can you imagine trying to live your life to a set of rules and regulations when you don't even know what they are? Occasionally, they can even change without warning.

Are you a saint or a sinner?
'A bit of both'

Are you a saint or a sinner?
'Neither'

It may appear to us that we are reading from someone else's book of rules but, whether we like it or not or even realise it, we create our own personal orthodoxies. The thing is – and this is very important, often underrated and overlooked – each of us has the ultimate say on whether we embrace particular beliefs, values and philosophies. Each of us carries the ultimate responsibility as to whether we choose to do or think something, be turned on or off, to love or to hate. That's what we all have: the ability to respond in any way we choose. That's what our personal sexual philosophies are all about: guidelines on how we choose to respond.

Imagine being able consciously to decide what your personal sexual philosophies are. Imagine writing your own deadly sins, virtues and commandments.

We've got to start somewhere, so let's begin with the seven deadly sins: pride, envy, gluttony, lust, sloth, anger, greed.

How do these fit in with personal sexual philosophies? Let's take a closer look at them and how they can influence us as sexual beings.

Deadly sin No. 1: pride

This one is also known as vanity. Like all of the seven deadly sins, pride is open to interpretation. Pride can be arrogance, conceit, self-complacency, self-sufficiency and these attributes can all be positive or negative. I had a friend who would take forever getting himself ready to go out, pampering and preening, making sure everything was just so. He could be seen proud and vain. That's how I saw him, but other women would fall over themselves to be near him. Excessive focusing on self can be seen as pride and vanity but can also be interpreted as looking your best.

'Excessive' is an important word. There is a line between being proud of something and being excessively so. Where we draw that line is the place that we allow pride and vanity to affect us sexually. The opposite of pride is humility and modesty, which, in all fairness, can be just as offputting as excessive pride and vanity. It's down to where you draw the line.

> **Are you a saint or a sinner?**
> *'Sinner with the heart of a saint'*

We are limited by pride or vanity when we hold onto past glories instead of acknowledging a job well done and moving on. This isn't the 'pride' we experience when we are genuinely proud of ourselves for a job well done. The limiting side of pride is that it holds us back.

Deadly sin No. 2: envy

Envy is the desire for others' traits, status, abilities or situations. Envy is meeting an old school friend as you are on your way home from the supermarket and she is on her way to a wonderful day out with her fabulous, rich friends. You have spent the last few hours buying food to feed your ever-hungry family and she is about to spend the next few hours indulging herself in amazing hedonistic pleasures.

Before you jump to any conclusions, who is the envious one? It depends on which side of the fence you are on. You may be green with envy at the thought of her spending a day doing exactly what she wants to without having to consider anyone else, but she may be seething inside, envious of the fact that you have a family and stability, which is something she would love.

Life is funny that way. The grass is always greener on the other side. A little bit of envy can be a good thing: it can give us the motivation we need to change our lives in some way. A lot of envy can be a real pain, as it can take the pleasure away from everything that is wonderful about you, your sexuality and your life right now.

Here's a thought: it doesn't matter who you are, somebody, somewhere is envious of you, looking at you from the other side of the fence, saying, 'I wish I had what they've got.'

Deadly sin No. 3: gluttony

This is one of my favourite sins. It is also a very subjective sin. For example, what kind of person is a sex glutton? Someone who has sex every day? Ten times a day? More than three times a week? It depends on your personal sexual philosophy, on where you draw the line. Personally, I'd rather have sexual gluttony than its opposite, sexual scarcity, but, when work takes me away from my nearest and dearest, I am more than happy with sexual scarcity.

Are you a saint or a sinner?
'I am now a saint, but I have been a sinner in my day'

But it's not only about the physical act of sex, is it? Our personal sexual philosophies embrace everything that concerns our sexuality. Which is just about everything.

Deadly sin No. 4: lust

We need lust. Without it there is no sexuality, only functional copulation. Lust is the craving we experience for the pleasures of the body. It doesn't have to manifest itself in the physical realm. Lust can lie in thoughts, in intentions, in words and actions. Lust can be subtle, almost imperceptible or it can be in your face and unavoidable. We are all little lust hot houses and regularly have lustful thoughts. Those thoughts aren't always about sex but they are always about desire, wanting things, power, sex, victory, whatever it is that gets your lust juices flowing.

The opposite of lust is indifference and I know which I prefer.

Lust gets its bad press from people who feed their fires of lust and keep them burning too hot for too long. They desire things, keeping themselves held in the state of lust that always remains unsated because they are always holding back. They end up stuck in the perpetual wanting, never allowing themselves to have the object of their desires. Come on, admit it, we all have lusty thoughts and these lusty thoughts can be triggered by anything – a picture in a magazine, a film, a book, a conversation, a dream, chopping carrots, all kinds of things. The only negative thing about lust is when we allow it to become an obsession or when we want

Are you a saint or a sinner?
'I am a saint – he thinks I'm a sinner'

something so badly that not having it makes us ill, yet having it is an impossibility. But you have the choice to walk away from lust when it weakens you, don't you? Walking away from something requires energy and the fifth deadly sin is a real energy eater. It's sloth.

Deadly sin No. 5: sloth

In today's busy, busy fast-paced world, sloth comes as a welcome relief. We need sloth – but what is it exactly? In its purest form, sloth is the avoidance of physical or spiritual work. It can also be described as laziness, idleness, inaction, inactivity, slowness or apathy. Sloth can be beneficial or damaging. Personally, I like a bit of sloth, because it gives me time to sit back and get my thoughts together. Sloth can be the ultimate de-stressor and can give us the free time we need to indulge in sexual indolence.

Are you a saint or a sinner?

'I pretend to be a saint, but I would like to be a sinner'

Sexuality isn't all about how far, how many, how long and how fast. Sexuality, when not used proactively, can simply be enjoying a state of slothful being. Sexually, sloth could be defined as opening ourselves up to exploring erotic potential that simply isn't there when we work to a fast-paced script.

What makes the difference between sloth = good and sloth = bad is all down to whether it is more beneficial to be doing nothing or to be doing something. Knowing the difference is what gives you the authority. Sloth becomes a 'bad' thing only when you are unaware that you can make a choice.

Deadly sin No. 6: anger

I've been trying to think of what use anger serves and I can't come up with anything. I think of all the angry people I know and try to figure out whether their anger has helped them in any way that I can't think of. We know they've got a short fuse and are very careful not to make them angry because, when they blow, they blow. When they're out of earshot, don't you talk about what a ridiculous, spoiled, pampered, pigheaded, bombastic person they are? If you are that angry person, watch out. We're all talking about you behind your back and none of it is lies.

Have you ever had an angry lover? They get angry about anything and everything. Angry people are always the victims, aren't they? Nothing is their fault. Their finger of blame points firmly outwards.

Are you a saint or a sinner?
'I can be both'

Anger makes an appearance in our personal sexual philosophy only when it is fuelled by jealousy, pride, frustration or impatience with faults. Why would anyone choose anger as part of a personal sexual philosophy? In its most primitive form, anger is to do with the desire to strike out – to externalise any bad feelings without thought for consequence. Fear, on the other hand, is the result of wanting to strike out but being afraid of the consequences.

Both fear and anger have at their root an insecurity about power. The question to ask is, where does this insecurity come from? That's one question I can answer easily. It comes from us, from me, from you. We create all the insecurities, jealousies, pride, frustration and power struggles that we think we can handle. Then sometimes we double it, just for fun.

There are times when we feel we have a right to be angry – it's true, we have a right to feel anger whenever we want – but remember, that holding on to anger gives power to the person or the thing that caused the anger in the first place. The moment we let go of the anger, we reclaim that power for ourselves.

Don't tell me that you've never felt angry at something and then spent the next few hours making yourself angrier and angrier? That's the great thing about anger: it serves absolutely no purpose whatsoever but sometimes, just sometimes, it makes us feel absolutely splendid.

Deadly sin No. 7: greed

Our personal sexual philosophies thrive on the seventh deadly sin. Greed is more than wanting material things or money. Greed is to do with eagerness, desire, longing, selfishness and wanting more than you need. There's nothing wrong with wanting more: Western society is built on the foundations of our wanting more.

Where does greed get all its bad press? Greed gets its bad name when it is teamed up with inconsideration for others. Eating a whole packet of biscuits is perhaps greedy but not bad. Eating a whole packet of biscuits when it should have been shared with others is greedy and inconsiderate. But what about context? Imagine you haven't eaten for three days and you find yourself among a group of people who are sitting down for coffee and biscuits. Everyone wanted a biscuit but they don't think you

Are you a saint or a sinner?
'Both, depending on my menstrual cycle, or amount of recreational drugs'

are greedy by eating the whole lot. They are only sorry that they couldn't find more for you to eat.

Context is everything. There is no such thing as a person who is greedy for sex, there are simply situations where it can be interpreted as greedy. Remember, greed only ever gets a bad name when it can be interpreted as being inconsiderate for others or self.

What have we learned from the seven deadly sins – pride, envy, gluttony, lust, sloth, anger and greed – presented as personal sex philosophies? They all boil down to personal interpretation. We can get facts, figures and statistics to say anything we want, depending on how we choose to interpret them. In the end, your personal sexual philosophy defines how you interpret things.

Sins are only *labelled* as sins. They were given this label 'sin' to signify that they were bad. But what is a sin? It is nothing more than a behaviour that you choose or don't choose to indulge in. 'Sins' got their bad press in the Christian world by association with the Devil, who's supposedly out there dangling these sins in front of us, constantly tempting us.

Are you a saint or a sinner?
'I like being a saint in public, but a sinner in bed'

The seven deadly sins are nothing more than choices. You are in control. You can choose to give the control over to someone or something else if you want, in which case you *choose* to give them control. You can choose to see the world as a sinful place or you can bathe in its glories, knowing that nothing is ever black or white, good or bad, right or wrong. It's all down to how you choose to interpret it.

Every choice we make has consequences for which we are ultimately responsible, not the Devil, not our parents, not our friends. It's me and you, ourselves.

And how do we make those choices?

Our choices are made by our desires.

Sex is ...
'where a man and a woman make love'

What does sex do for you?
'Makes me feel good'

When I feel sexy, I ...
'desire sex/touch myself/partner/fantasise'

Sex is ...
'what two people do'

When I feel sexy, I ...
'reach out and touch him'

I wish for ...
'money'

I know ...
'it never lasts long enough'

Does love play a part?
'I prefer it when it does'

Sex is ...
'wonderful – if you have the time for it and have a loving partner who will fulfil your needs as well as his own, hopefully not before yours!'

What do you believe about sex?
'I believe that it is a natural act and is totally confused by various media, religious and social groups so that most people, including myself, never really unravel what it is and what it matters. It is often used as a tool to get what people want, a tool for power, and has a monetary value.'

I want to feel ...
'beautiful'

7

Desires

So, what fans the flames of your desire? What makes the difference between fulfilling your desires and not igniting those flames?

I know what lights my fire and I know what makes the difference between my being fulfilled and being unfulfilled. But I can't even begin to tell *you* what to think and how to react because there is no one right or wrong way to suit everyone. It's not a question of 'one way fits all'.

Wouldn't it be great if they made a little pill that we could take to sort out our tangled love lives and keep our libido at exactly the right level? This remedy could make us feel desirable and loved, give us the power to make wise choices and refine and improve our logical thoughts so that we would never make irrational decisions or think unreasonable, inconsistent and insane thoughts.

I want ...
'plenty of sex with just one man'

This one little pill would sort out your sex life, make things run smoothly, and you would never have to bother yourself with desire or making choices. Would you take it?

What I love about sex is that it *is* an irrational, illogical, inconsistent thing. It is a thousand different things to a million different people.

Have you ever had anyone tell you that the only way to enjoy sex is to relax? And yet haven't you ever had amazing sex when you were so worried that you would be discovered that you could hardly breathe?

I want ...
'to have fun'

When it comes to sex, nobody can tell you what you should or must do, what you ought to be feeling, or what you can expect. You are the one who makes the choices and, when it comes to desire, these are governed mainly by your internal state and the level of your desire. For example:

- 'I want to make love in the shower before we go to work, but I can't be bothered' – ('I want to make love' = desire; 'can't be bothered' = internal state)

- 'Sometimes I want to have sex a different way but I'm too shy to ask' – ('I want to have sex a different way' = desire; 'I'm too shy to ask' = internal state)

- 'It's Wednesday, I'm feeling horny and I'm getting laid tonight' – ('I'm getting laid tonight' = desire; 'I'm feeling horny' = internal state)

Internal states can totally overrule any desires.

Imagine for a moment that you are walking down the street minding your own business and you bump into the most gorgeous person you have ever met in your life. Your level of desire goes through the roof:

'I want that person, I want them now, I want to rip their clothes off with my teeth, oil them up and have my wicked way with them right there on the pavement and I don't care who's watching.'

We've all seen that person, had those thoughts, and resisted. Your desire says, 'Phwoar! I want sex with him/her, right now.' Your internal state says, 'I would be too embarrassed. There are people watching and I might get arrested.' That's your controlling internal state pouring cold water on those desires. If it hadn't been for your internal state suddenly going all bashful, you could be there right now, writhing and grinding.

I want ...
'sexual equality'

So what are these internal states? Where do they come from and what can we do about them? An internal state is a state of mind that reflects how you feel at any given moment. For instance: sad, happy, amorous, flirty, tired, apathetic, angry, horny, on top of the world, down in the dumps, frustrated, utterly satisfied.

What causes them? Anything can trigger them but there are some common misconceptions surrounding internal states:

Misconception 1

The first misconception is that internal states control you. Have you ever heard yourself saying, 'I can't do that – I'm too tired'; 'I can't help myself – I'm feeling so horny'; 'Sometimes I can't control myself – it must be the wild thing in me'? The fact that you are tired, horny, scared, happy is not the reason why you can or can't do something.

Misconception 2

The second misconception about internal states is that other people always seem to grab all the good ones and you are left with the short straw: 'How come *she's* always so bloody happy and chirpy and I feel miserable and irritable all the time?'; 'She really seems to enjoy herself when she goes out and *I* always seem to have such a bad time'; 'I very rarely feel aroused but *he* can feel sexy at the drop of a hat.'

It's not as though there were a limited number of good internal states that we all have to fight for and the losers get stuck with the duds. Internal states don't run out of stock or wear out. You choose whichever you want.

Misconception 3

The third misconception is that, once you wake up with a particular internal state, you're stuck with it for the whole day: 'I got out of the wrong side of the bed – it's going to be one of those days.' If you went downstairs and there was a letter on the doormat telling you that you had won the lottery, that might change your internal state, don't you think?

Misconception 4

Many people are under the impression that external influences can change your internal state for better or for worse: 'I woke up this morning, got out of the wrong side of the bed, felt shitty, went down-stairs and I'd won the lottery – I feel fantastic!' It's not the external influence that has changed your internal state but your *response* to the external influence.

Misconception 5

'It's just not fair …' And what's fairness got to do with anything?

Misconception 6

There's nothing you can do to control your internal state.

Ah, but you can. You are the driver, the pilot, the director, so it is totally up to you to decide whether the fact that you're tired means that you can or can't do something.

I want …
'to be fulfilled'

If you want to feel good or bad all the time, the only person who has ultimate control over your mood is you. If you are in a bad mood, people may attempt to get you to change your mood but, ultimately, you have the last word on whether you lighten up or wallow. If you happen to get out of the wrong side of the bed – the only person who maintains that bad mood all day is you.

External factors don't cause us to feel a particular way: we somehow select an internal state and anchor it to some external influence such as a look, a laugh, the weather, a car, a phone call or a person.

If you accept that you are in control of your internal states, how come they override your desires so often? What causes that situation and why is it that we can get all hot-blooded over something or someone and have cold water poured over it by an internal state that pops up out of nowhere?

The wonderful, amazing thing about us humans is that we are magnificent, sublime, complex beings who are not satisfied with a simple approach to our sex lives. Wouldn't it be easy if we could go through life saying, 'I want sex, fuck me' or, 'I don't want sex, fuck off'?

I've got some chickens in my garden and that is their philosophy. They waddle up to one of the cockerels and let them know they want to be jumped, or the cockerel struts up to his chosen one with that look of intent in his beady little eye and they either have sex or they don't. They don't fret about what everyone else might think; they don't feel bad if they get turned down. They just shrug in their chickeny way and think, 'Next!'

So why can't we be more like chickens? Because our brains are bigger, and we can understand concepts of guilt, shame, rejection, power, bliss, fun, strategies, torture, orgasm, other people, sexual politics; and because we are each, in our own personal way, sexual eco-warriors.

And what is a sexual eco-warrior?

The 'eco' I am talking about here is a set of considerations that affect us on conscious and subconscious levels. Any potential sexual situation we find ourselves in that requires an ounce of deliberation will see

our sexual eco-warrior spring into action, bombarding our sub-conscious with questions that we either react to or ignore.

What sort of questions and considerations are introduced by this sexual eco-warrior aspect of my nature? Here's a few:

- 'Am I OK with this?'

- 'Are others OK with this?'

- 'What are the positive and negative effects of this?'

- 'What is this an example of?'

- 'What is the purpose of this?'

- 'What will I gain or lose if I do this?'

- 'What will or won't happen if I do this?'

I want …
'to be more experimental'

Although you may not realise it, this is what is running through your head at the same time as desire. This is the ecology script regurgitated by your sexual eco-warrior self, to protect and preserve you from possible mishaps.

The sexual eco-warrior part of ourselves asks these questions and then assesses the situation, sometimes as quickly as the time it takes to say, 'Phwoar!' Most of the time we don't even realise that these complicated calculations are being carried out. If you were to stop for a moment, step back and observe your love life, sex life or sexual feelings, you would see patterns emerging. Any recurring themes such as rejection, frigidity, bad decisions, fantastic lovers, no lovers, blissful relationships, serial dating, monogamy, pregnancy, one-night stands or marriages are themes that you have introduced into your life. You may not even be aware of it because it is the sexual eco-warrior within you that has decided these are the results you need.

This is one reason why we tend to get famously uninhibited when we get drunk. The sexual eco-warrior shuts down and leaves you to it.

I want …
'*more raunchy, seductive sex*'

The sexual eco-warrior within us can be seen as a do-gooder, or a do-badder, depending on how we choose to calibrate it. Most of the time, we don't even realise that we are continually fine-tuning the sexual eco-warrior within. Every time a thought materialises, deep, deep down our sexual eco-warrior is taking note of the thought and acting upon it.

What kind of thoughts are we talking about? Thoughts such as:

- 'I don't want to get hurt again'
- 'I want to feel attractive'
- 'I need stability'
- 'I need excitement'
- 'I want someone I can call my own'
- 'I don't need anybody'
- 'I want revenge'
- 'I just want to be loved'

The moment one of these thoughts pops up, the sexual eco-warrior sets to work with its litany of questions, and then calibrates a suitable response.

I want ...
'spoiling and adoration'

By way of demonstration, let's imagine for a moment that I have decided, for whatever reason, that I don't want to be hurt in a relationship. I'll run through those questions, answering as a sexual eco-warrior with my best interests at heart:

- 'Am I OK with this?' 'Totally OK because I don't want to get hurt.'

- 'Are others OK with your not getting hurt again?' 'Oh, yes. They really don't want another week of my sitting there, weeping and wailing.'

- 'What are the positive and negative effects of this?' 'The positive effects of not getting hurt mean I will be a happy little bunny. The negative effects will possibly be a narrowing of experiences. But so what? I'm safe.'

- 'What is this an example of?' 'Not wanting to get involved with heartless bastards again.'

- 'What is the purpose of not getting hurt again?' 'Self-protection.'

- 'What will I gain or lose if I do this?' 'If I never get hurt again I will feel comfortable and safe.'

Now, it took me about ten minutes to think of answers to the sexual eco-warrior's questions, yet the sexual eco-warrior itself comes up with the answers in a moment and acts on those answers in the most logical way it can.

If I were consciously to come up with a solution
for my 'not getting hurt again' conundrum,
I might decide to be more selective in
my choice of partners or decide to go for a
totally different kind of partner or even to
marry the next person I met because he'll be
mine, he won't be able to leave me and I
won't get hurt.

I want ...
'to be understood'

But the sexual eco-warrior within us doesn't always tell us how it's
operating. It may interpret the data gathered as:

> Doesn't want to get hurt. Hurt = feelings. If I feel nothing I won't get
> hurt.

Or:

> Doesn't want to get hurt. Hurt happens in a relationship.
> Relationships start when two people are attracted to each other. If I
> make myself unattractive, I won't get into a relationship and I won't
> get hurt.

Or:

> Doesn't want to get hurt. Hurt is caused by somebody hurting me. If I
> hurt them first, they can't get to me.

These aren't necessarily choices that you would ever make consciously but the sexual eco-warrior within us does exactly what it
feels is best to protect you as it's got nothing else to go on. You've
written the guidelines, it only acts on them.

It acts as a conscience, like a little Jiminy Cricket, keeping us on the straight and narrow, except that it is *our* straight and narrow, nobody else's. It is we who lay down our own law, and our sexual eco-warrior makes sure we adhere to what we consider to be our law.

So, what defines these laws that we write for ourselves to govern our desires?

I want …
'to be younger – I want to go back and start again'

Desires are choices that cannot be made by logic alone. All choices have consequences for which we are responsible. The implications of the choices we make need to be looked at carefully, since these are choices made by desires. The consequences of choices from desires can affect our lives at many levels, not only the carnal. The choices we make are a reflection of our values and our choices mirror the kind of person we wish to become.

Whoever thought it was all so complicated? Let me read through that last paragraph again:

Desires are choices that cannot be made by logic alone. Yes, I understand that. Desires, on the whole are pretty illogical things.

All choices have consequences for which we are responsible. So we make the choices, we take the glory, or take the flack.

The implications of the choices we make need to be looked at carefully, since these are choices made by desires. But if it works for you, there's no need to fix it.

The consequences of choices from desires can affect our lives at many levels, not only the carnal. So always carry a condom and if he says he's just about to leave his wife – don't believe him.

The choices we make are a reflection of our values and our choices mirror the kind of person we wish to become – a nun, a harlot, a sophisticated man-eater, a happy wife, a career woman, or perhaps all of the above.

Now you know why sometimes it's so much easier to say, 'Not tonight, dear, I've got a headache.' It gets the old sexual eco-warrior off the hook.

When we start making excuses for ourselves, for our thoughts and actions (I'm too old; I never do that sort of thing; I'm worried about what others might think of me; I was drunk), aren't we letting ourselves off the hook? Do we need to find excuses for ourselves? Can't we make our way without excuses? Can't we make our way without tripping up on our own obstacles?

I want ...
'to feel wanted and secure in my present relationship'

Yes, we can.

I'm too ...
'scaredy-cat'

I wish for ...
'hugging and kissing'

I'm too ...
'much of a slapper according to my friends'

I know ...
'just to relax and enjoy yourself'

Good sex is ...
'when both you and your partner are in the moment at the same time and you totally lose yourself in the act of sex and don't care who walks in or what is going on around you – like fire alarms'

I know...
'sex is good'

What does sex do for you?
'Not a lot at my time of life'

Sex is ...
'indicative of what is going on in my life, sometimes boring, humdrum, sometimes inspiring and fantastic'

Sex is ...
'messy, powerful'

The best time for sex is ...
'night-time, in the dark'

I wish for ...
'orgasms'

I'm too ...
'cautious'

8

Power, Satisfaction, Stability and Sex

The obstacles and excuses we put in our way are either caused by us or cause us to have certain feelings, but do we need to find excuses for ourselves? Can't we make our way without excuses, without tripping ourselves up?

Believe it or not, our feelings and emotions about sex are all motivated by three basic conflicts and desires: sexual power, sexual satisfaction and sexual stability.

How can sexual power, satisfaction and stability motivate feelings and emotions? And what has the desire for sexual power got to do with my thoughts and actions concerning sex?

'I ... love **sex, but** ... *I also love chocolate'*

Before I start delving into the issue of power, I want to shed a little light on the subject of desire. If I desire something, it's something I want that I don't at this moment in time have.

A desire for sexual power suggests we are powerless or that we need to make things happen in a particular way, for a particular reason.

On a personal level, desire for sexual satisfaction means wanting to feel satisfied or the awareness of feeling in some way unsatisfied either physically or emotionally. On an interactive level, a desire for sexual satisfaction is also concerned with wanting to be loved, to be liked, to be cared for, to be approved of or admired.

'I ... *love* **sex, but** ... *don't get enough! Kids!*'

When we desire sexual stability we want to feel as though we have some security in our lives. We want this when we feel threatened or insecure or are suffering from lack of confidence and need to feel steady and safe. I'm not talking just about stability within a relationship. We don't all need or want a stable relationship, but we all need to feel some kind of sexual stability within ourselves. This is the stability that comes from knowing that if we do a certain thing at a certain time, we will get a particular result.

The desire for sexual power, sexual satisfaction and sexual stability is the foundation of every sexual feeling we experience.

These three desires maintain whole belief systems that we hold about sex and sexuality. When you think about it, either we desire sexual power, sexual satisfaction and sexual stability or we already have them. There is also another side to this coin. Sometimes we seek actively to relinquish sexual power, to deny ourselves sexual satisfaction and to avoid sexual stability, not necessarily all at the same time. However, whether we desire them or avoid them, sexual power, satisfaction and stability are still the three things that motivate us.

These three motivating factors are also the keys to the way in which we relate to our lovers. Looking at them one at a time, we see how they work within a relationship.

Sexual power

This isn't to do with the 'dominant/submissive' power trip, although, when pushed to the limits and exaggerated, it can be. Some of us habitually give sexual power to our partners, sometimes without even realising, never taking the initiative, never making the first move, being happy to let them do all the work and always letting them choose how and when to have sex. These are all signs of submitting to their power. But remember: when we find ourselves in this situation, we have chosen to let the other person take charge. We have bestowed upon them that power and we have chosen to be powerless – and therein lies our power. It's all a bit Zen, isn't it?

'I ... *love* **sex, but** ... *sex isn't everything*'

There are other times when we take charge of the power, assert ourselves sexually and use that power to get what we want. It doesn't matter whether we use sexual power in an active or passive sense. The bottom line is, if you're not getting what you want sexually, you ain't using your power in the right way. I am not about to get on my soapbox and tell you the right way to use your sexual power. I am not you and I don't know what you want. If you are happy and comfortable with the division of sexual power between you and your partner, then put a gold star by 'sexual power' – you're sorted. However, if you feel that something is amiss, experiment with where the power lies. Have a go at taking charge, or give them the power – you can always take it back again. If you find yourself unhappy because you feel you've become a doormat or a sex tyrant (and some of us love being either, or both), remind yourself that this is a choice you have made and that it is within your power to do something about it.

> 'I ... *love* **sex, but** ... *like to have the lights out*'

There is another equation in the theme of sexual power. It's not that necessarily one has the sexual power and the other hasn't. If you choose to relinquish your power, it doesn't mean you are powerless. Being powerless carries it's own kind of power. The only right scenario is the one that suits you and possibly your partner too.

Sexual satisfaction

Allow me to use two cultural icons to illustrate this particular motivational force: Mick Jagger and Yoda. He's the little wrinkly guy in *Star Wars* who trained Luke Skywalker to become a Jedi (I'm talking about Yoda).

Now what did Jagger sing about satisfaction? 'I try and I try and I try and I try ... I can't get no ...'

And what did Yoda say on the subject of trying? 'There is no try, there is only do or don't do.'

Close your hand into a fist. Trust me for a minute, I'm not losing the plot, I'm demonstrating the concept of 'try'.

Close your hand into a tight fist.

Done it?

I'm going to assume that you are sitting there with one hand clenched into a fist.

'I ... love **sex, but** ... *I don't want to get pregnant'*

Now, try to open your hand.

Done it?

If you are sitting there with an open hand, you are not doing it right.

Start again. Close your hand into a really tight fist and try to open it. Really try. Is it open yet? If your hand is now open, you have opened it but not *tried* to open it. Trying to do something involves thinking about it, pontificating, procrastinating, skirting around the issue and not really committing to doing it. *Trying* to do something involves expending energy in unworkable ways to make it happen, or making no real effort to succeed at all. Bearing all that in mind, close your hand into a fist and *try*, really *try* (remembering the definitions of try) to open it. Is your hand still closed? Good, you have successfully tried. Now, open your hand. There, that was easy, wasn't it? Good old Yoda – he knew what he was talking about. 'There is no try, there is only do or don't do.'

If you are still a bit unclear or resistant to the issue of 'try', run these ideas by yourself for a moment:

- 'I will *try* to make sure I am sexually satisfied'; 'I will make sure I am sexually satisfied'

- 'I will *try* to satisfy you'; 'I will satisfy you'.

When it comes to sexual satisfaction, don't try: either do or don't do.

If you have a desire for satisfaction and you aren't getting any or enough, then what's to be done about it?

The usual response when we want to fulfil the desire for sexual satisfaction is to concentrate our efforts on what's wrong. It's easy to pinpoint things that are going wrong, but remember: we get what we focus on. So when we focus on what's wrong, what's not happening and how unsatisfied we are, that sows the seeds for more of the same. It's time to change our tactics and get more (or some) sexual satisfaction. Instead of focusing on the dissatisfaction or what's missing, find out what needs to be added, changed or left out. Experiment with new combinations, new approaches, different energies, and do things differently.

Sexual stability

Some of us crave sexual stability; some of us fear it. Stability can also mean unchangeability, security, durability, steadfastness and, as a concept, can be something we long for or run away from. We sometimes shy away from sexual stability because we are afraid that something bad might happen or it might turn out to be a big mistake. It can also seem boring and predictable or we can't see the point, as it will never last, anyway. The avoidance or the search for sexual security can make us scared, out of control and desperate.

'I ... love **sex, but ...** sometimes it ruins a perfectly good relationship'

Have you ever had the sense that you are becoming sexually secure and felt afraid or have you ever felt anxious that something is about to upset your sexual security? If you have found yourself in either of those situations, did you struggle with yourself or your partner, even though there was nothing to struggle against? Did you feel like running away, or doing anything you could to maintain the status quo or find yourself deliberately or even unconsciously sabotaging a good thing? Join the club. We've all done it, this is what the desire or avoidance of sexual security does to us: it can turn us into irrational crazy folk.

'I ... *love* **sex, but** ... *I've never had an orgasm'*

Here's the rub: whether you crave sexual stability more than anything else, or whether you dismiss it as a boring, stultifying, imprisonment, sexual stability has you in its clutches. You can run but you can't hide.

Whether we like it or not, sexual power, sexual satisfaction and sexual stability are the driving forces behind our sexual self-control and self-confidence. At the same time, they can also be the initiating force behind any sexual imbalance, destructiveness or loss of control and they are the reason we maintain outworn habits, ideas and self-limitations.

Once we face up to the things that drive us sexually, we can start to be aware of our urges and handle them with strength and insight, rather than letting them rule us. We take control of our sexual power, sexual satisfaction and sexual stability. *They* may be the vehicle that drives our sexuality, but *we* are the drivers of the vehicle. We're not

'I ... love **sex, but** ...
*not everything that comes
with it*'

all on the same road, going in the same direction with the same intention, but, wherever we choose to go, we want to be successful in getting there, even if we choose to go nowhere.

That takes strength, which is what the next chapter is all about.

9

Sexual Strength

Sexual strength is very different from sexual power. They can be differentiated in this way: Sexual power comes from determination, direction and the values we hold about sex, whereas sexual strength comes from beliefs – what we believe about sex, what we believe about ourselves and what we believe we are capable of. These beliefs fuel our inner strength.

The opposite of strength is weakness. Sexual strengths and weakness are both good and bad, depending on their context. Your sexual weakness can be your strength and your sexual strength can be your weakness. It's not a clear-cut, black-and-white issue. It's not even shades of grey. It is all down to perspective, the views we have and our beliefs about a given situation at a particular time.

What do you believe about sex?

'It has the means to create life and should not be taken lightly'

So let's take a look at beliefs. Every person to whom I ask the question, 'What do you believe about sex?' gives me a different answer. I have been asking many people questions about sex and sexuality while writing this book and I have been getting some very interesting and illuminating answers. One thing I discovered is that whatever it is that people believe about sex forms the basis of their experience of sex. It can be a bit of a chicken-and-egg conundrum – which came first, the bad sex or the belief that sex is overrated? It's amazing, isn't it, how some people can dip their toe, metaphorically speaking, into the world of sex and decide that the water is far too cold and they ain't never going to swim in that particular stream and enjoy it?

While I'm on a swimming metaphor, indulge me for a few moments and allow me to wallow a little more. I went swimming one evening recently and, for me, swimming is fun. I bob about in the pool, I throw balls around, I have splash fights, I laugh a lot and I love being in the water. That's what I believe swimming is all about and that's the fun I get when I go swimming. There were some people in the pool who took their swimming very seriously. They swam up and down, up and down, in a regular and ordered fashion. For them, swimming is repetitive exercise and that's what they got. When I go to the beach, I see people who dip the very tip of their toes in the waves and decide it's not for them. It's far too cold and wild for their liking, and that's exactly what they get: cold, wild, inhospitable water. So they don't want to take the plunge.

What do you believe about sex?
'Different generations have different approaches'

Then there is my friend who trained as a competitive swimmer. For her, swimming was something she did at five o'clock every morning for two hours and seven o'clock every evening for two hours. She told me that there was no pleasure in it, as she had abandoned the pleasure in pursuit of excellence and chlorine-bleached hair. She believed she had to work hard to be the best. That's what swimming was to her – hard work, for a purpose.

If we are to believe all that we read in books and magazines, good sex is possible only if you have the agility of a gymnast and the body of a supermodel, and both partners are achieving multiple orgasms.

I don't know about you but people have told me that they've had good sex when they have looked like the Michelin man, they've had amazing sex without orgasms and even managed wonderful sex without moving a muscle. Some people also admitted to having fantastic sex completely on their own.

It's got nothing to do with what you read in books and magazines, but it has everything to do with what you believe about yourself, what you believe you are capable of and what you believe about sex.

What do you believe about sex?
'Everything, blow jobs and anal sex and everything'

On the subject of sex and sexuality, what do you believe about yourself? These beliefs are your strengths and also your weakness. It's time for some soul searching. Maybe you know what you are supposed to believe; maybe you are aware of what others tell you to believe. This isn't for anything or anybody else: this is for you. There's only me and you here, so dig deep into your heart, into your soul, into your sexual being and give yourself some answers.

- What do you believe about yourself?

The answers may come easily but, if they don't, here's another approach. Say to yourself:

- When it comes to sex and sexuality, I believe that I am …

Scribble down whatever comes into your head – words, phrases or images that come to you, however strange they may seem. Make a note of them and keep going until you can't think of any more. Writing it all down helps us to remember what popped into our heads because sometimes our mind tends to be selective in its recollection of certain things and forgets others it may consider inappropriate.

When you have finished this first soul-searching exercise and while we are still on a roll, let's dive straight into the second question:

- On the subject of sex and sexuality, what do you believe you are capable of? Say to yourself, 'I believe that I am capable of ...'

Don't simply churn out what you think people want to hear. Nobody else ever has to hear or read your answers. Write them on loo paper and flush them away afterwards if you must or throw the paper away, burn it, press 'delete' on your computer keyboard. This is for your eyes only and the only person you need to answer to is yourself. Go for it, have fun.

What do you believe about sex?
'I believe that sex is the biggest part of marriage'

You are finding out about your strengths and your weaknesses. Dig deep and discover your inner sexual self.

Right, we've done the foreplay, so to speak, so this next question is the biggie:

- What do you believe about sex? Say to yourself, 'I believe ...'

What else do you believe? And what else?

Keep on going until you run out of answers. Some people can fill the back of a postcard, some can fill a notebook, so, whatever is right for you, go for it.

I am assuming that you have your lists, sets of notes or answers. Have a look at your answers. Do you see any themes developing?

What do you believe about sex?

'It's closeness and happiness between you'

Some people have a tendency to answer in the negative: 'I believe that I'm not ...' or, 'I believe that this isn't ...' or, 'I believe I can't ...'

If you find that you are one of those people, take a look at your answers and see if you can put them in a positive way. For example, 'I believe I'm ... not shy.' If you aren't shy, what are you instead? Bold? Daring? Brave? Confident?

'I believe that sex is ... not all it's cracked up to be.' You've told yourself what it's not, but what *is* it? A disappointment? A physical act between two people? Something that needs spicing up?

'I believe that I am capable of ... attracting a partner if I could only lose some weight.'

I'm not letting you get away with answers like that, either. Don't let yourself put any conditional words and phrases on your beliefs. Conditionals are words and phrases such as 'when', 'if', 'if only', 'soon', 'as soon as'. Conditionals effectively put a limit on your strengths. Using the example above, notice the difference in the strength in these two statements:

- 'I believe that I am capable of ... attracting a partner if I could only lose some weight.'

- 'I believe I am capable of ... attracting a partner.'

Here are some more examples:

- 'I believe that sex is ... good, but only when I relax.' 'I believe that sex is ... good'

- 'I believe that ... my sex life will get more interesting soon.' 'I believe that ... my sex life will get more interesting tonight.'

Can you see the differences?

Take another look at your answers. Are your beliefs founded upon your fears? For example, do you believe that good sex is impossible? What would your sex life be like if you believed that good sex was possible? Your beliefs about sex are the things that give you your sex drive and, if these beliefs are founded on things you fear or worry about, then this is what your drive will focus on.

Strength doesn't have to be about aggression, force, competitiveness, defensiveness or struggle. Strength is about belief in yourself and what you are capable of. Sexual strength has as much to do with affection, tenderness, intuition and direction as courage and control.

What do you believe about sex?
'I believe that emotion and love can help make sex better'

When we have a clear sense of our sexual strength, we are able to be in control of our passion, which doesn't mean we squash it or subdue it.

When I sit behind the wheel of my car, I am totally in control. I can rev up the engine, I can drive like a crazy speed freak or I can crawl down the road at a snail's pace. I can drive straight, or swerve from side to side. I am the boss. I know where I want to go, how quickly I want to get there and whether I want to go straight there or take the scenic route. I also have the ultimate control of whether I go it alone or take someone along with me. If there is someone travelling with me, I can choose to let them decide on the route or take them on a mystery trip. I can follow the same route we always travel because we love it or because it's easy and needs no effort to plan, or we can plan and prepare a special journey together.

What do you believe about sex?

'I only believe how good it feels when I'm actually doing it'

I also have certain responsibilities in mind, being a sexual eco-warrior. It's important to make sure that nobody gets hurt as a direct result of my actions and that anyone who is on the journey with me is there because they want to be. I want them to feel comfortable and enjoy the journey too.

Being in control of our passion, our sexual urges, our sexuality, is the thing that ultimately gives us freedom and sexual strength as well as a sense of honour, reliability, honesty and purpose. Once we are able to overcome our fears about our beliefs, then any weaknesses we have become our strengths. Otherwise, our sexual weaknesses turn into self-indulgence, a sense of defeat and unworthiness, or simply a confusing clash of interests. And why on earth would we want that for ourselves? We are the ones driving our car. It's up to us, to each individual one of us, to make sure we can enjoy having control of our passions. Sure, temptation in all its forms exists, but we also carry within ourselves the strength to avoid it or give in to it. It's up to us.

Sometimes, it's difficult to avoid getting sucked into focusing our attention on petty concerns and it's always easy to forget that the strongest energies we possess are tenderness, kindness and gentleness. Think about it: if we use our strength only through force, then we will always come up against conflict and resistance. There must always be a winner and a loser. Real strength comes through tenderness, kindness, gentleness, courage and self-discipline.

What do you believe about sex?
'I believe it's a natural expression of love'

Let's return to the car metaphor. I crashed my car recently. It was raining and I collided with a van travelling in the opposite direction on a blind corner. Nobody was hurt but the last thing I wanted to do after the crash was to drive down that road again. Unfortunately, that road leads to everywhere I want to go and, to get anywhere, I have to face that blind corner.

I got in the tiny little courtesy car and drove that road again, this time being extra careful on the bend. I didn't let the past restrict or smother me: I learned from it and it gave me a deep respect for my own limitations.

Sex is …
'having it off with your husband!'

I am …
'fed up with the way women are portrayed'

I need more …
'loving and affection'

I want …
'acceptance and to have people to see me as who I really am rather than who I was and past pictures I may have painted of myself'

What do you want from sex?
'To lie back and do nothing and let my partner get a sweat on'

What do you believe about sex?
'I believe that you need to have a degree of maturity – the more old-fashioned are the most sensible. Free love doesn't benefit women.'

I want to feel …
'hot'

I want to feel …
'cared for'

When I feel sexy, I …
'kiss his neck'

What does sex do for you?
'Nothing at the moment'

I want to feel …
'outrageous'

I need more …
'sensuality'

10

Respecting Limitations

The best way to deal with the past is to learn from it and move on. The best way to move on is to realise what your limitations are and, if you can't change them and won't fight them, respect them.

What are these limitations we impose on ourselves and how do they get there? We all have different ones, don't we? How do we come to have our individual beliefs, values and limitations?

Our minds are learning machines. We are born with an insatiable appetite for discovery. We take in information about everything that happens to us, everything we experience, everything we see, hear, taste, feel and smell, then choose to accept or disregard this information. Most of the time, we are completely unaware of this filtering process. This sorting out of information and sensory input forms the foundation of our beliefs, values and self-imposed limitations. Our subconscious mind isn't satisfied with leaving it at that – oh, no. It builds on these foundations, making them stronger, adding texture, decorating, reorgan- ising and clearing away unnecessary or

'I ... like **sex**, but ... *will only take part if they love me'*

contradictory information until we have an arrangement that suits us and fits in with our beliefs, values and self-imposed limitations.

It's like having one of those TV makeover teams permanently on call.

Let's play with that idea – here's an example. You let it be known to your TV makeover team lurking in the deep recesses of your mind that you don't like giving oral sex. The makeover team set to work, throwing out any information you may have stored in your mind about what is good about giving oral sex. They rip out that metaphorical oak-carved fireplace that reminded you of how much you enjoyed giving your partner pleasure and nailed in its place a huge MDF creation with 'Yuk! Yuk! Yuk!' spray-painted on it. They furnish this space with things to remind you to dislike giving oral sex and keep updating these reference points regularly.

'I ... like **sex, but** ...
it makes a mess'

Now, imagine instead that you let it be known to this dutiful makeover team that you love giving oral sex. This time the team will race to fill the space with things that reinforce your enjoyment. They may still rip out the old oak fireplace, because that's what TV makeover teams always do, but this time they will spray-paint 'Yes! Yes! This is great!' all over its MDF replacement. They will fill the space with images, sounds, memories, anything and everything that can reinforce the enjoyment factor.

Unlike the TV makeover teams, where you have very little say in what the central theme will be, you tell your inner makeover team precisely what to work on and they do it, to the letter, sometimes a little too literally.

Like the TV makeover teams, yours will throw out anything that doesn't fit in with the scheme of the makeover, no matter how useful or cherished it may be. Irrespective of whether it is a belief, a value or an ornament, if it adds conflict or dissonance to the general ambience and effect that is being created, it is out on the scrap heap.

Unlike the case with the TV makeover teams, we can't turn off the TV and walk away. We carry all these ornaments and decoration, the good and the bad, around in our heads all the time.

What thoughts would you like to change? The only things that need throwing out are those thoughts and beliefs that limit us in ways we don't want to be limited. Maybe you feel that your thoughts and beliefs about sex need a complete overhaul. Maybe you would like to improve things a little and get rid of some ideas you had that were useful to you in the past but limit you now. Before we start redecorating, let me say a few words about limitations.

'I ... like **sex, but** ... *can't find anyone I like enough to do it with*'

Some of our beliefs limit us. They prevent us from achieving our sexual potential, but we all have some real limitations that can't be changed. If you are tiny, believing that you are tall won't make you any taller. Believing that size is a limitation will *turn* it into a limitation, but believing that size won't limit you will free you.

Respect the real limitations and be aware of the limiting things created by your imagination.

Some of us believe that we will never have a meaningful relationship or that we can never have an orgasm, or that we are too ugly/stupid/shy/young/old or whatever. These beliefs carry with them 'proviso' beliefs, which go something like this: 'If only I were/if only I had more/less ..., then I'd be able to/I wouldn't have to ...'

'I ... like **sex, but** ... *only on a weekend*'

When we begin to look closely at what we believe about sex, we can become aware of any beliefs we hold that keep us back from where we might want to be, limit us or contain us.

So what do you believe about sex, about your potential as a sexual being?

It's an easy question to ask but a bit of a sod to answer. All our lives we have been told things about sex by our parents, friends or lovers, from books or by the all-invasive media.

Do you believe everything you've been told over the years? Have your beliefs changed? What do you believe about sex now?

Your answers form the foundations of who you are sexually and present the sexual comfort zones within which you are prepared to live. Some of us operate within very tight sexual comfort zones.

A sexual comfort zone is a self-imposed imaginary line that, once crossed, makes us feel uncomfortable. Our sexual comfort zones can be built with many things:

- 'Touch me there, I feel good; touch me there and I don't like it.'

- 'I love it when you talk to me like that; when you use those words, I feel uncomfortable.'

- 'Doing it this way feels great; doing it that way is a real turn off.'

A sexual comfort zone provides the difference between what arouses you and what turns you off or leaves you cold.

Sexual comfort zones are not clearly fixed, set in stone or even clearly marked. They can change, shrink or expand rapidly or even fluctuate from moment to moment, depending on the context. For example, you may enjoy and feel perfectly comfortable when your partner strokes your bottom. It feels good, it hits all the right spots and you might even enjoy it if they give you a flirtatious, sur-reptitious rub while out in public. If anyone else tries rubbing your pert little behind, even though they might do it in exactly the same way as your partner, they would probably end up with a black eye because it would put you way outside your comfort zone.

There's a lot of talk about 'needing to expand our comfort zones' but, when we are perfectly happy with them and they serve a useful purpose, cherish and enjoy them.

Not all self-imposed limitations are bad. All of them serve a purpose. The comfort zones we wrap around ourselves are there to protect as well as limit us. The answer is to get rid of the self-imposed boundaries that hold us back from where we want to be and develop a deep respect for the limitations and com-fort zones we set ourselves that keep us feeling comfortable.

'I ... like **sex**, **but** ... *not the soreness*'

If you find yourself saying, 'I wish I were more ....' or, 'I wish I were less ...', then have a go at expanding or contracting your comfort zone. Allow yourself to feel a bit more comfortable with whatever you want more of and let yourself feel a little bit uncomfortable with whatever you want less of. I use the term 'a bit' deliberately here. It's easy to change things 'a bit'.

What is it that prevents us from changing, from narrowing or expanding our sexual comfort zones? If, for example, your wish was 'to be more adventurous sexually', you may manage to make the switch to feeling totally comfortable with *anything*. One moment you were a five-minute-quickie-in-the-dark type of person, the next you're swinging naked from the chandeliers, yodelling and leaping on anything with a heartbeat. You can certainly aim for that, if you fancy the idea, but take it a bit at a time. It's not an all-or-nothing, famine-or-feast thing: it's degrees of deliciousness best discovered a step at a time.

Possibly the worst thing we can do, if we have one of those 'I wish I could be more/less …' moments, is to do nothing. Some of us feel it's impossible to change, or perhaps we feel we don't really need to. Maintaining the status quo is often far easier than daring to consider that change could be possible. Maybe you think you have to dare to recognise that you can choose to change.

'I … like **sex, but** … *I'm more inhibited than I should be'*

It all depends, I suppose, on whether you feel there is a problem. A problem is nothing more than the gap between where you are now and where you would like to be. Nothing is actually a problem unless you decide it is, unless you bestow the title of 'problem' on a situation.

If you feel you have a problem, is it getting in the way of where you want to be? If not, then there's no problem. It can be as easy as that.

Beliefs, values, limitations, philosophies, thoughts and ways of life will continue to grow and shape us as long as we continue to feed them and give them life. As long as we make space for them and make room for them we make sure nothing is there to dilute them. I'm not just talking about the negative stuff – this works both ways. Irrespective of whether they are self-imposed limitations of a positive or negative kind or dearly held beliefs, once these things cease to be of use or we find something more useful, they are out of our thought processes faster than you can say, 'Take me baby, I'm yours.'

'I ... *enjoy* **sex, but** ... *don't always have enough time*'

That's the wonderful thing about sex: there is always something new to learn, a new phase of sexuality to pass through. Our sexual comfort zones fluctuate and change as we re-evaluate our thoughts.

The only thing that can be said about sexual comfort zones with absolute confidence is that they will not be the same in five years' time. I'm not talking about sexual comfort zones as a mass collective thing here: I'm talking specifically about *individual* comfort zones.

Think back five years. Think how your sexual comfort zones have changed over this period of time. Perhaps they have become smaller and tighter; perhaps they have expanded and softened. Five years is a pretty random timescale but it's long enough to see a difference. Go back ten years if you want convincing.

'I ... *often desire* **sex,** **but** ... *realise I'm too tired for it*'

It is impossible to label a large sexual comfort zone as a good or bad thing or a small comfort zone as a good or bad thing. It depends entirely on the context and your personal needs and wants. If your sexual comfort zone supports you where you want to be or if you feel the need to give your sexual comfort zone a bit of a makeover, set your inner makeover team to work and transform it. Go on, ask them – they'll jump at the chance.

Don't forget that old saying (paraphrased here), 'Change what we can but only if we want to. Accept what we can't change or don't want to change. And wait until we can tell the difference, before we let in the makeover team.'

Sex is …
'a good way to burn off a few calories without going to the gym!'

What does sex do for you?
'Makes me feel happy'

Good sex is …
'It can be the lovemaking but also the fast and the furious'

'Talking about sex is like talking about your salary: it doesn't matter how much you earn you always walk away from the conversation feeling you are somehow not getting paid enough.'

Good sex is …
'when you feel this unbearable need for him that can't be satisfied any other way but with sex'

What does sex do for you?
'It puts a smile on my face and keeps me happy for a while'

I need more …
'romantic sex'

What do you want from sex?
'Presents'

I'm too …
'fat to feel truly sexy, but am working on that'

I wish for …
'orgasms and oral pleasure'

I know …
'I will have good sex someday'

I'm too …
'expectant'

11

Everything Changes

One thing is certain in life, love and sex: everything changes, nothing stays the same and there's no such thing as good or bad change, only different perceptions of how change affects us.

Change can be daunting, although it is the *thought* of the change that is scary, not the change itself. When change happens, usually we are too busy dealing with it and reacting to it to be frightened. Change can be exciting, stimulating and life-changing, or it can be barely noticeable.

Does love play a part?
'Sometimes yes, but on occasion no'

While I was researching this book, an older woman told me about what sex meant for her. She said, 'In my younger days with my husband, it was wild, exciting, passionate, hot and often. Now we rarely have sex and that's got nothing to do with not loving each other. Our needs have changed. Being close and knowing that we are happy together is enough for us now.'

Being curious, I wanted to know if she could pinpoint a time when this change took place.

'It happened gradually over time. It wasn't as though we woke up one day and found we didn't want to have sex with each other any more. The passion gave way over time to companionship and I like it, it suits us.'

Does love play a part?
'Yes – definitely'

Another older person told me that he ran a business with his wife for forty years and, when they retired from the business, they stopped having sex. This worried them. They wanted to continue their sex lives but, for one reason or another, couldn't.

These couples were the same age and going through the same diminishing sex life change, but had been affected differently.

Change happens within relationships that can alter the thoughts and feelings you have about sex. These changes within a relationship don't always happen gradually. We can be a red-hot, steaming love machine one minute and a chance remark or incident can change us, in a heartbeat, into a cold, inhospitable iceberg.

Our thoughts about sex also change at each stage of relationship building. Relationships don't come ready-made, they have to evolve and be built by the people involved in the relationship. There are many different ways that a relationship can evolve – here's one example:

The first stage is attraction. We are attracted to somebody and men-tally we try them on for size and fit. We may have noble thoughts about the other person and what they can give us or we may have an overwhelming desire to have wild sex with them. The central theme at this stage is, 'I am attracted to you.'

A precursor to this first stage is the search for a partner. This need to search can manifest itself in a number of ways. There could be an obvious gap in our lives that needs filling or it could be part of a game we play with ourselves or others. Don't tell me I'm the only one who has ever taken on a bet with their best friend to see who would be the first to pick up a man for the night. A relationship can be as superficial as that, if that's what you want at a particular time. In my young, free and single days, I would spend evenings out with my friends seeing who could chat up the ugliest or most boring bloke, who was bought the most drinks – in fact anything that amused us at the time. We weren't bothered about having sex with these men. The thrill was in the chase, a bit of harmless fun. However, there comes a point when shallow and meaningless is no longer enough – we want more. Our needs change and we want a 'proper' relationship. We want to start having sex or having a different kind of sex.

Does love play a part?

'Always; it's better if it does'

The second stage in relationship building is desire. This is where the 'other person' becomes the pivotal point around which our world turns. When that person is with us, nothing else matters; when they are not with us, all we want is them. This is the 'butterflies in the stomach' stage and anyone who has ever experienced it knows what I mean. That other person becomes the focus and the colour of our life. Everything else becomes dull and distant by comparison. But here's the rub: all this moons and Junes, hearts and flowers, walking on air and being unable to think of anything but that person doesn't automatically become a reciprocal thing. To the object of your desire you might be nothing more than someone they are attracted to at that shallow and meaningless level. You might even be someone they have been out with for a bet or they may not even be aware you exist. Sometimes life's like that.

Every now and then, desire fires from both sides and it truly makes you feel glad to be alive. That's when the desire stage can make way for the learning stage – we learn what they like and want and we teach them what we like and want. This stage can last as long as the relationship because, as we are always changing and altering, what we like changes and alters.

We learn what others teach us and it's not always the lovely stuff. For example, if I have a relationship with someone and treat them like a doormat, walking all over them, acting like a total bitch, being hurtful and demanding, and they choose to stay with me, then I learn that they are willing to put up with whatever I throw at them. Let's imagine they stand up to me one day and ask me to change my ways. They want to be treated with kindness and respect and want me to show them occasionally that I love them. I could look at them with contempt in my sparkling violet eyes and say, 'Yeah, sure, babes, whatever you say' – and still continue being Superbitch.

If they do nothing, then I learn once again that I can get away with it. If I feel like it, I can start a campaign of terror in the house because they have taught me that they will offer no resistance. I also learn that, if ever they do pack up their things to leave when I have been particularly bad, I can weep and wail, make promises and even modify my behaviour for a while, and they will stay.

Does love play a part?
'Depends who you are'

Now, let's rewind and go back to where our long-suffering partner is asking for a little respect. 'If you don't do this,' they might say, 'then it's over, I'm leaving.'

> **Does love play a part?**
>
> *'Definitely ... without love it becomes an act of fun'*

If I don't modify my behaviour and they don't leave, they have taught me that their attempts at standing up to me are not to be taken seriously.

If I don't give them the respect and love that they have asked for and they leave, as they warned me they would, then I've learned the hard way that they're not willing to put up with my tyrannical behaviour.

A lot of what we learn from and teach each other isn't always the good stuff. If I were to put up with third-rate sex without taking the initiative, making suggestions or complaining, then I've taught my partner that I'm willing to settle for less.

In relationships, real learning and teaching take place through experience, demonstration and example and by taking the initiative occasionally. What have you got to lose? Three minutes of huffing and puffing once a fortnight? Surprise your partner occasionally and they'll soon learn. Teach by example. If you want more adventurous sex, be a little more adventurous. If you want some raunchy stuff, be a little raunchy. If you fancy a quickie, tell 'em they've got five minutes.

So, you're teaching them what you want them to learn – what happens next?

Love. Actually, love can happen at any time during relationship building – love at first sight, or first contact at least, certainly exists. Love, for many of us, is the ultimate aim for a relationship. It is, after all, the cement that binds us together; it is the icing on the proverbial cake; it can be the cake itself but not always. Love can play a very minor role within a relationship or have no role at all. It depends on the relationship and what we want from it.

When I have been talking to people about sex and I ask them, 'Does love play a part?' the overwhelming response is 'Yes.'

Once those flames of passion have been ignited and allowed to burn, eventually they subside and we are left with glowing embers. These glowing embers of passion allow us to change and grow and the flames can be fanned back at any time.

> **Does love play a part?**
> *'There has to be love to connect fully'*

Once we are in a relationship, we become aware of the fact that a relationship is more than simply something we experience with another person. The term covers the relationship we have with a lover, with the world, with ourselves. The relationship changes and evolves continually through these different points:

- You change your philosophy, your body, your energy levels, your responsibilities, your outlook on life, your needs, your wants, your desires, your beliefs and your sense of belonging. In fact, anything and everything.

- Your partner changes, perhaps in similar ways to you, perhaps on a completely different trajectory.

- The world changes. The seasons, geography, time, politics and fashions are all constantly changing and evolving and affecting us in some way.

- The relationship as an entity in itself changes. A relationship that is beautiful, perfect and all-consuming when the lovers are alone in private may be a thing of shame in a different context. Context is everything.

Does love play a part?

'Yes, if the sex is to be good'

Can we change and the relationship stay the same? Any change in ourselves or our partners, no matter how small or insignificant, causes a change within the relationship. As a relationship changes, the sex changes. It fulfils different needs.

What causes these changes? Can we stop them? Is it possible to find the ultimate relationship and maintain it?

Imagine you have just had the best sex of your life. It was everything you have ever dreamed of and more. You are feeling breathless, energised, fantastic and completely satiated. Now, imagine that you want to have exactly the same experience again. So you recreate the situation exactly: same person, same time of day, same place, same positions, everything. Would it be the same? I hate to be the one to break it to you but, no, it wouldn't. For one, you have already experienced it, so your perception of the event will be different. Even if you attempt to recreate it the moment you have got your breath back, time has passed and time, as they say, changes things.

I am not saying that you can never have sex as good as that again. Trying to recreate exactly that same experience may give you an experience that is even better, or as good as the first time, but it can never be the *same*.

Every minute of every day, our mind is taking in information on whatever is going on around us and, in order to accommodate that information, it has to make slight or massive rearrangements to all the things it has already stored. Our mind is an incredible learning machine and it assimilates everything. As a result, we are constantly evolving, even though it sometimes happens in a confusing way.

With all learning experiences, whether conscious or unconscious, occasionally confusion sets in. A wise old sage once told me, 'Confusion is the first step towards understanding.' When we find ourselves saying, 'I can't understand it – we've done everything in exactly the same way as we did it last time, yet it is somehow different', we can start to look at and discover what else has entered the equation. We can then begin to form an understanding of those unseen or unnoticed events that shape who we are, who our lover is and how our relationship is evolving.

Does love play a part?

'Love does play a part now, but it doesn't have to'

When you think about it, sexuality is a function of thought and perception. We are constantly updating, expanding and revising how we see the world, ourselves and our feelings about sex, even if these updates and revisions pass unnoticed.

The statement or definition of who we are and how we experience life is continually changing, but are we always at the mercy of change and fate? What if we want to change something? Are we completely powerless?

Powerless? Nothing could be further from the truth. Change is inevitable but the doors are wide open for you to change things in any way you choose. You can be active in making changes in the way you want because things are going to change anyway, whether or not you want them to, so why not play an active part in the plan? If mentally you plot your progress, you can congratulate yourself later on how instrumental you were in changing something.

How do I plot my progress? Do I need charts? Special equipment? A video camera?

No, although I'm not ruling them out as possibilities if that's your sort of thing. Simply ask yourself (and answer) a few simple questions:

- 'Where am I now in relation to the change I want to make?'

- 'Where do I want to be?'

- 'What's stopping me from being there?'

Does love play a part?
'Not always. Sometimes it's more about fulfilling a biological urge'

Bear in mind that plans can and do go astray: kids get ill, cars break down, shit happens, life's like that. It's how we *react and respond* to change that can make or break us. Life is about change, change is about growing, growing is about adapting and evolving and evolution is what we do best.

What do you want from sex?
'Sometimes I want a sensitive connection, other times I want a way to fall asleep and forget about my worries. I sometimes want it to be meaningful, hearts-and-flowers, L-O-V-E sex, but other times I want fast and dirty sex which reminds me that as a woman I am powerful.'

What do you want from sex?
'Lots of it'

I want to feel ...
'like sex every night'

When I feel sexy, I ...
'take off all my clothes and annoy him'

I wish for ...
'loving'

Sex is ...
'sometimes a pain in the arse because the guy is always thinking about it and always wants to do it'

I know ...
'that love is a powerful thing'

I wish for ...
'a woman'

I'm too ...
'horny; naughty (years ago)'

I wish for ...
'foreplay'

I'm too ...
'sexually active'

12

Changing Points of View

Like it or not, we all make judgements about people, situations and all that life throws at us, and we make these judgements all the time. The process of judgement and evaluation isn't fixed and it isn't set in stone. It varies according to who we are, where we are and how life's twists and turns affect us at any given moment. One evening, you could be having passionate, unhurried sex that feels so good and so right that you never want it to end. The next, that same passionate unhurried sex could be so tedious that you wish it would be over quickly so you can sleep. It's not that the sex or your partner was any different or that you loved them any the less on the second night – maybe you were simply dog tired.

What do you want from sex?
'Mind-blowing pleasure – at least twice!'

A different perspective can alter how you judge things. We often impose our judgements on others, don't we? 'You must be getting tired now …' 'If I were you, I'd …' 'Aren't you ashamed? I would be …'

A judgement is a criterion for a point of view. Nothing more, nothing less. As soon as we judge something (and we're doing this all the time, usually without even realising), we compartmentalise it, name it, put it into a particular box and make a decision about it. What's more, this seemingly complicated process can take place in a matter of seconds.

On what do we make judgements? Anything and everything.

How do we make these judgements? This depends on our criteria – what we are looking for at any given time. For instance, if we are looking for a potential lover, we might run a mental checklist to see how they measure up.

First things first: how they look. Obviously, if the initial meeting is not face to face, other factors come into play, but when we meet potential partners in the flesh (and, if you're actively looking, everyone and anyone could be a potential partner), the first thing we check out is whether they look right to us. The wonderful thing is that we all like different types. There's no such thing as one-size-fits-all when it comes to relationships.

Once we've formed an opinion of a potential partner based on the initial meeting, we can delve a little deeper and see if their personality measures up to our original assessment. I can't be the first person in history ever to spot a fine-looking man only to politely and quickly back away as soon as I've entered into conversation with him and realised how dull he was.

What do you want from sex?
'Connection'

We can override judgements: 'Looks like a Greek god, talks like Muffin the Mule – no thanks'; 'Looks like a virgin, talks like a misogynist but has the most amazing house in the country – I'll give him

What do you want from sex?
'Excitement'

a whirl.' 'I don't usually go for that type of person, but there's something about them that turns me on.' Everything depends on our personal criteria.

We set up our personal judgement criteria and then our subconscious does the most outrageous things to support these judgements.

What kinds of things does it do? First, it twists or bends things and forgets or ignores things. When we really want to stick the judgmental knife in, we can support our judgements in an expansive, all-inclusive, vague and inaccurate way.

How do we do this?

First things first: twisting and bending facts. We twist and bend things to support our sometimes erroneous judgements by occasionally claiming to be a mind reader:

- 'I know you fancy her.'

- 'You think about sex all the time.'

- 'You never consider my feelings.'

How do we know these things for sure? We don't – but we're prepared to do a little selective guesswork to support our judgements.

We also twist and bend things by interpreting two separate experiences as being equivalent to each other:

- 'He doesn't want sex with me any more – he's always watching the television.'

- 'She can't possibly fancy him: he's so ugly.'

How does the fact that he's always watching TV mean that he doesn't want sex any more? How does the fact that he's ugly mean that she can't possibly fancy him?

What do you want from sex?
'Honesty and stability'

We apply value judgements to sex all the time.

- 'That's perfect ...'

- 'It's wrong to ...'

- 'It's so good ...'

Whenever we say these kinds of things we are making value judgements. Remember the unwritten ending – '... according to whom?'

- 'That's perfect ... according to whom?'

- 'It's wrong to ... according to whom?'

- 'It's so good ... according to whom?'

We often impose our judgements on others, don't we? For example, have you ever caught yourself saying:

- 'You must be getting tired now ...'

- 'If I were you, I'd ...'

- 'Aren't you ashamed? I would be ...'

All examples of imposing your judgements on someone else.

We can reshape completely unrelated things so that it appears they are one and the same:

- 'She doesn't love me – we never talk any more and she falls straight to sleep after sex.'

- 'She really loves me – she falls asleep in my arms after we have sex and we don't need those endless discussions any more.'

Unwittingly, we can also twist things by implying that one thing causes another. For example:

- '*If* you do that to me, *then* I'll be putty in your hands.'

- 'When you talk to her, *it makes me* angry.'

- 'He's late again – *that means* he doesn't care about me.'

What do you want from sex?
'A baby'

We can support our judgements by twisting facts or making links with unrelated actions but there are other, easier ways of making judgements and keeping those judgements alive. Very often, we choose selectively to forget things or omit contrary facts. How do we do this? By using sweeping generalisations:

- '*Everybody* does it like this.'

- '*Everything's* fantastic.'

- 'I would *never* do that.'

- 'That's *all* they *ever* talk about.'

Any time we use words such as 'all', 'every', 'never', 'everyone', we strengthen our judgements with generalisations.

- 'Everybody does it like this.' *Everybody?*

- 'Everything's fantastic.' *Everything?*

- 'I would never do that.' *Never?*

- 'That's all they ever talk about.' *All? Ever?*

When it comes to sex, we have an opinion on everything. We judge ourselves, our partners, other people, the act of sex itself – in fact, there isn't one nuance of sex that we don't have an opinion about. We support these judgements with comparisons, expectations and generalisations, and we twist or bend things in order to reinforce our judgements. We forget things selectively or omit evidence to the contrary and we can back our judgements by viewing any particular aspect of the world in that all-inclusive, vague and inaccurate way.

However, our opinions and our judgements about sex, about anything, are just that: our own opinions. The same applies to the judgements of others because, make no bones about it, you will be judged. One person may think you were the best lover ever and another will think you were nothing more than a lump taking up valuable bed space. They'd both be right. It's their judgement, their opinion, and they own them. You and your lover could be in the same space, sharing the same sex together, but you can never share each other's mind.

What do you want from sex?
'A good time and a sense of belonging'

We don't only twist things to support negative judgements. We can also keep those rose-tinted spectacles of ours firmly in place with a few well-positioned twists, generalisations and omissions.

The important thing with judgements is to learn how to think clearly and cultivate a balanced viewpoint. Justice isn't possible without respecting fairness and truth as important principles rather than nice behaviour that we adopt because we want to be liked.

> **What do you want from sex?**
> *'Security and to be the one'*

On issues concerning sex, beware of being too liberal with the truth. Some truths are inappropriate for particular situations. Imagine this scenario:

> You want us to be totally honest with each other? OK – your breath stinks, you're not the best lover I've ever had, you grunt like a pig, you've got a small dick and when I orgasm it's more through luck than any involvement you had in the process. Despite all that, I love you. Isn't it good that we can be totally honest with each other? I feel so much better now. How about you?

Some judgements are best kept to ourselves, or at least stored away should we ever need them for revenge.

Remember the ecology that is concerned with how our thoughts and actions affect those around us? Bear this ecology in mind when imparting your judgements to others and when judging yourself. When you find yourself saying, 'I wouldn't dare do that', ask yourself, 'What would happen if I *did* dare do that?' Suspending a judgement every now and then can open doors to all kinds of possibilities.

Step back and get a wide-screen version of a narrow viewpoint when you need to, because a narrow viewpoint can seriously cloud a judgement.

For example, I used to think that only beautiful people with perfect bodies could have fantastic sex because that was the conclusion I came to from watching Hollywood movies. It was only when I allowed myself to step back a little and listen to normal people telling me that they had fantastic sex that I realised my judgement about 'Hollywood glamour equals fantastic sex' was a rather narrow viewpoint. I opened my eyes and it opened up my world.

It's so nice occasionally to allow ourselves to see the world as it is, permitting ourselves to accept things rather than judge them. Not all the time and not with everything, just now and then have that little glimpse of the world not as you would like it to be or fear it is, but observe it objectively, free from opinions and prejudice.

What do you want from sex?
'Enjoyment, affection and security'

This may seem a frightening thing for some of us to do, because it can feel as though we are relinquishing control and abandoning all that we previously held sacred.

What does sex do for you?
'Makes me feel like a queen – on top of the world! And it makes me feel needed and loved.'

I am ...
' horny quite a lot because I'm pregnant'

I am ...
'nervous around people I find attractive'

'I ... love sex, but ... I haven't always'

What do you want from sex?
'Orgasms'

What do you want from sex?
'I want to be good at it'

I want to feel ...
'respected'

I know ...
'I was loved'

I wish for ...
'a free afternoon once in a while'

Sex is ...
'fucking immense'

What do you believe about sex?
'I believe that sex is a special gift as well as an animal thing and has unpredictable results (though that's probably 'cos it's been a long time since I had regular sex with one person).'

Does love play a part?
'Love is greater than the ecstasy of sex'

I want to feel ...
'happy'

13

The Martyrs' Club

What would happen if we were to relinquish control and abandon everything that we had previously held sacred? We're not talking about a total about-face. This has nothing to do with turning nuns into sex fiends or turning a warm lover into a frigid hater.

If it's working for you, don't attempt to fix it; but, if you feel a need to change some aspect of your sex life, then begin by learning to release the judgements you make about things you want to change.

When we become tied by our beliefs, values, expectations and judgements, we limit ourselves to experiencing things that fit them. This is fine when we don't have a problem. If your sex life is everything you want it to be and more, then we can safely assume that your beliefs, values, expectations and judgements are doing the job they're supposed to and keeping you happy.

If there's anything you're not happy with, it's not the end of the world. You still have choices. You can choose to put up with it, ignore it or choose to do something about the situation.

I'm too ...
'choosy (as in too many expectations)'

If there are things we're not happy with and we do nothing, then we end up being a martyr, suffering for what we believe in, martyring ourselves in order to uphold things we consider to be sacred in some way.

So how exactly do we martyr ourselves? We put up and shut up. We complain to people who can't or won't do anything to help. We pretend that everything's fine. Jealousy can turn us into martyrs and, whether it is jealousy of a lover's attentions or jealousy of our own abilities and feelings about sex, it is always based on feeling inadequate in some way. Think about the last time you experienced sexual jealousy in any form. As you look back, can you see how it was founded on a misguided belief that you were somehow inadequate? For example:

I'm too ...
'scared'

- 'I'm jealous of the attention my lover gives to others.'

- 'I'm jealous because other people get more sex than I do.'

- 'I'm jealous of anyone who can experience multiple orgasms.'

'Inadequate' is a harsh word but jealousy comes from feeling that we are somehow worth less than the things we are jealous of. Jealousy can be destructive. Let it go and move on. You are the most magnificent person you know and jealousy is for martyrs.

Fear can also turn us into martyrs. We deny ourselves experiences and feelings because we fear the consequences. We let opportunities pass by for fear of losing what we've already got. Fear can be a good thing and it can be that little voice in the back of your mind that keeps you safe, but, if there's no danger and you still hold onto fear like a talisman to protect you from imagined harm, then welcome to the Martyrs' Club.

I'm too ...
'inhibited'

Self-loathers can also have unlimited access to the Martyrs' Club. Believe it or not, there are people out there who don't like themselves, or do like themselves but not their sexual selves. This self-loathing, this lack of self-worth, gives them *carte blanche* to deny themselves what they really want, to shy away from pleasure or even to experience pleasure as a punishment because then it will support their beliefs and values about themselves.

Self-loathers are easily recognised by the things they say: 'I don't deserve anything nice'; 'Nothing good ever happens to me'; 'I'll never manage to find someone willing to put up with me.' Self-loathers can feel that they're not acknowledged in some way or feel as though they have somehow betrayed themselves. Everything becomes coloured by their misapprehensions.

Just as there are no set rules concerning feelings of jealousy and fear, self-loathing martyrs can hate themselves for anything: 'I love him too much'; 'I don't love him enough'; 'I hate myself because I can't stop thinking about sex'; 'I hate myself because I never get aroused'; 'I hate the noises I make when I have sex'; 'I hate myself because I can't really let go'; 'I hate myself – I'm too fat'; 'I hate myself – I'm too thin.'

I'm sure we can all think of people who fit into this category. If you recognise yourself as a self-loathing martyr, don't hate yourself for it. Read on and lighten up.

When we love someone, we love them warts and all. We accept those little faults and foibles that make them who they are. The moment we start to loathe some aspect of them, however small and insignificant, we begin to focus on it. It becomes bigger and takes over until we become incapable of noticing how wonderful they are because all we can see is the irritation.

People who can't or won't learn to love themselves, who don't feel comfortable enough to really love who they are, warts and all, are choosing to be martyrs. After all, if we can't love ourselves as the magnificent sexual beings we are, how can we expect anyone else to love us?

I'm too ...
'boisterious, people say I scare them'

It's a strange thing but, when we start to focus on our perceived shortcomings, we erect imaginary barriers to keep people and pleasure away. Weird as this world is, it is often those things that we hate most about ourselves that turn our lovers on. The 'warts' that we might choose to hate could be the very things that fascinate and attract others.

To maintain their misery, martyrs can get very creative with the ways in which they choose to suffer. Some martyrs suffer in silence and nobody is even aware they are suffering. Others tell anyone and everyone of their woes, inviting pity. The more they cling onto their suffering, the greater the hold it has on them.

- 'My lover wants to have sex first thing every morning.'

- 'My lover can't keep his hands off me.'

- 'I haven't had sex for ages.'

Whether you are a martyr or a non-martyr, you initiate others' reactions by the way you think and act. If you want to martyr yourself for whatever reason, the easiest way is to invite pity.

- 'My lover wants to have sex first thing every morning – pity me.'

- 'My lover can't keep his hands off me – pity me.'

- 'I haven't had sex for ages – pity me.'

Martyrdom is a state of mind. It's possible to make any statement about yourself and tag on a 'poor me, pity me' to achieve the desired 'victim' effect, but, if you think about it, that same phrase can be transformed by tagging it with something that will allow you to free yourself from the mantle of martyrdom.

I'm too …
'talkative during sex'

- 'My lover wants to have sex first thing every morning – what a lovely way to wake up.'

- 'My lover can't keep his hands off me – he still finds me attractive.'

- 'I haven't had sex for ages – but that doesn't mean that I'm not a sexually vibrant person.'

The 'poor me, pity me' approach can have its advantages, though. It can keep things the way they are. It can allow us to maintain the status quo. If we were to release ourselves from our self-imposed martyrdom, where would we go? We would have to go somewhere, do something, change the situation somehow, and we all know that sometimes it's easier and a lot less effort to keep things the way they are.

Occasionally, a member of the Martyrs' Club feels an undeniable need to break free of their shackles. They realise that all of this moaning and complaining, this fear, jealousy, self-loathing and suffering have prevented them from growing, moving on, from embracing the joy of life. They feel the need to change and, for change to happen, something has to be sacrificed. Have you ever been there? I know I have. I can think of a hundred examples of where I've stopped myself from having pleasure because I was clinging to fear, jealousy, self-loathing or suffering. Sometimes this was a good thing, (for example, protecting or keeping me safe), but there were other times when I was simply afraid for no logical reason.

I'm too ...
'old now'

If we allow ourselves to adapt to changing circumstances by letting our thoughts and preconceptions become flexible rather than rigid, if we are willing to suspend our judgements occasionally, then sacrificing one thing to obtain another becomes easy.

We can respond to change in many ways. Sometimes we feel that we can't adapt and we continue to cling to the past, holding onto all those negative emotions that help maintain the status quo. When we set ourselves up as a martyr, particularly a sexual martyr, it is often as a protective device.

It's a fact that opening ourselves up to life and all its potential glories can hurt, but shutting ourselves off through martyrdom can dull the pain until we feel nothing. Sexual martyrdom is all about indulging ourselves in our own problems and it doesn't matter whether those problems are real or imagined. Once we are able to see situations without pretence, we can move on.

If we free ourselves from martyrdom, if we put ourselves in a position where we can take a fresh, unbiased look at our feelings about sex, what happens then? What about that 'dark side' that has been kept suppressed by our martyrdom? What happens if we open the floodgates and sexual fantasies, sexual impulses, rude and dirty thoughts take hold of us?

I'm too ...
'set in my ways'

That all depends on whether we welcome them or not, or whether they surface at inappropriate times.

Good sex is …
'when both you and the person you're with can laugh and have fun in a serious way'

Sex is …
'about feelings you show to others, but it can be just sex'

What does sex do for you?
'It revitalises me and gives me more energy'

The best time for sex is …
'afternoons'

I am …
'most of the time sexy and confident'

The best time for sex is …
'when you're feeling horny and when it's spontaneous, especially in the morning'

Does love play a part?
'Hopefully'

What do you want from sex?
'To be satisfied, loved, needed and to be ridden until I sweat!'

I'm too …
'tired most of the time'

I want to feel …
'like I am the centre of the universe at that moment. I want him to look me in the eye and feel like nothing else is filling his head but me'

14

Genies Out of Bottles

Imagine for a moment that you have no experience of sex, have never had a rude thought, have lived in a sex-free cocoon all your life, like a genie in a sex-free bottle – and somebody has just popped the cork. Here you are, exploding into a world filled with anything and everything you can imagine sexually. The world is your oyster. You can do whatever you wish and you have no preconceptions and no prejudices. What would you wish for?

There's no point in saying, 'I wish for everything – give me the lot' because that would open the floodgates for everything, good and bad. So, if you were that genie, trapped in a sex-free bottle, and had just been released into the world of sexual pleasures, what would you wish for? Apart from the precondition that you can't wish for everything, what would you wish for sexually and how would you go about getting it?

I need more ...
'attention and praise'

Whenever we begin a relationship, we are like that newly liberated genie. We have the opportunity to look at sex from a fresh perspective and make whatever we want happen.

I need more ...
'slinky undies'

I don't know about you, but I've never yet met anyone who would consciously wish for a dull and boring sex life, or who wishes to feel like a drudge or wishes they had less pleasure.

What sort of things *do* we wish for? We wish for fun, for excitement, for love, communication, desire and a hundred other things, all different but each with a strong positive undercurrent. In our world of genies and wishes, dullness and drudgery don't even get a look-in.

With a new relationship, we can be whoever we want, we can redefine who we are and what we want and need, sexually. We can be a genie and say to our lover, 'What do you wish for?' and then find out what they want and what turns them on, and tell them what we desire. Think about it: we can remove all our old obsolete patterns and start afresh. We can get rid of all the old thoughts and behaviours that kept us from where we wanted to be and look forward to new possibilities, new ideas and new situations as well as a new lover.

We can do this. It is perfectly within the realms of possibility to wipe the slate clean with each new relationship and reinvent ourselves. But do we?

There's nothing to stop us waking up each morning and deciding that things have got to change, and changing them. I'm not talking only about changing ourselves with new relationships. We can change an old, comfortable, familiar relationship into something new and exciting, or make a wild, exciting relationship occasionally into something more gentle. We can change something that is mind-numbingly boring into something that gives us a reason to get up in the morning. We can make our wishes, stake our claims, make a difference – but do we?

On the whole, we tend to be pretty bad at being genies. We don't like to make a fuss, we don't like to make demands. We all have wishes, but, as for making them come true, that's for dreamers, isn't it? Besides, it's easier to stick with the old patterns, isn't it? Even if they don't give us exactly what we want, sticking with the tried and tested is so much easier and much less effort than granting ourselves wishes that may or may not evolve into something wonderful.

What if it all goes horribly wrong and we lose everything? What if we make fools of ourselves? What if these new possibilities don't give us what we want and we lose more than we gain? What if we thought it was going to be easy and fun so we go for it and it turns out to be difficult and dull?

I need more ...
'hours in the day'

OK, Genie, I've popped your cork, what are you going to wish?

- I wish ...

- I wish I could be ...

- I wish I could have ...

- I wish my lover was more ...

- I wish to have less ...

- But what if ...?

Almost everything we could wish for is within the realms of possibility, yet we put up these 'but what if …?' barriers to prevent ourselves having our wishes. That's a good thing because, if automatically we had everything we wished for, life would become much too easy. Don't genies offer a simple caveat as they grant their wishes? Don't they say, 'Be careful what you wish, because you may get exactly what you ask for.'

I have a hypothesis: all these 'but what if …?' tags that, habitually, we put on the ends of wishes are actually a sophisticated filtering device masquerading as neurosis.

Let's play for a moment and try out my new hypothesis. I'm a genie in a sex-free bottle who's just popped out into the world of possibilities. What do I wish for? 'I wish I could be a total sex goddess.'

I need more …
'romance, cuddles'

Wham, bam! Allerkazam! Behold, one total sex goddess living it large and causing mayhem.

Now, let's just rewind a moment and allow my what-if filtering device to refine that wish somewhat: 'I wish I could be a total sex goddess – but what if I couldn't cope with the constant attention that undoubtedly I would attract? Could I come to terms with being a "mum" and a "total sex goddess"? Do goddesses ever slob out and watch TV all night? What if my life changes so radically that I simply can't deal with it?'

This is where we think about what it is we really want, so we start to modify the first wish a little: 'I wish I could have a hot sex night once a week and on that night I could be a total sex goddess.'

Let's check out the what-ifs:

- 'What if my partner doesn't like it?' That's simply not going to happen. It would be his dream come true.

- 'What if the kids wake up?' Could be a problem.

- 'What if I modify my wish a little more and have a hot-sex morning once a week when the kids are all at school and I can be a total sex goddess?' Sounds good to me.

- 'What if the phone or doorbell rings?' Don't answer it.

- 'What if I enjoy it?' Top ho.

- 'What if I don't enjoy it?' Put a tick on your list of 'things I've tried' and move on.

And, if you don't wish for anything, nothing will change. That's not necessarily a bad thing, but it should be the best you can make it, given the constraints of real life.

These what-if filters allow us to tailor our wishes to suit our individual lives. I know this is an obvious statement but we are all different with different lives and different wishes. I can't give you guidelines on what to wish for because I'm not you, I don't know where you are at this moment or where you want to be heading.

One thing is certain: in order to make changes, improvements in life, something has to give way. In order to include new possibilities, ideas or situations in our lives,

I need more …
'gorgeous and intelligent men'

we have to sidestep some of the old, ineffectual possibilities, ideas and situations. That's a good thing, isn't it?

There does come a point where we have to transcend those what-ifs and either do it or don't do it. Either way is fine, as long as it moves us away from where we don't want to be and in the direction of where we do.

But what if we know something needs to change but can't be bothered to do anything about it, for whatever reason, and stay put? We end up stuck in a rut of sexual inertia. Sexual inertia is fine for some of us and, if you feel comfortable in that state, enjoy it. However, there are times when sexual inertia ceases to be comfortable and becomes dull and boring. That's when we get the urge to change things, when it's just not fun any more.

The best way to combat sexual inertia, laziness, stagnation or depression is to make yourself move from your rut. The first stage is recognising that you are in a situation that needs changing – which is half the battle. At this point, you are faced with choices. Either you can do something about it or do nothing and let things remain the same. But they won't, because you are now aware of the situation and have identified that something isn't as you want it to be, so there's no turning back.

I need more …
'foreplay'

Remember the philosophical postulation about Schrödinger's cat? Let me tell you about it (as I recall it with artistic licence). Schrödinger's cat is a theoretical pussycat that has been put in a soundproof box. It may or may not have been poisoned and may or may not be dead or seriously ill. You have no way of knowing what state the cat is in until you take a look. You could sit outside the box and assume that the pussy is alive and well or make any assumptions you like about what is going on inside the box. However, the moment you open the box and take a look, everything changes. The facts are there in front of you. You have ascertained that the cat is in fact in the box, that it exists, that it is alive and well and grateful to be set free. Or perhaps opening the box confirms that the pussy is in need of attention and may be saved if you can give it what it needs to get better. Maybe it's dead. Who knows? One thing is for certain: unless you look inside, sooner or later the pussy will die, possibly from the poison that it may or may not have eaten, maybe from inattention and loneliness, definitely from thirst and hunger.

Once you have identified that there is something in your life that you are unhappy with, everything changes, irrespective of whether you take action or not. It may happen in an explosion of undeniable action, or it may be barely perceptible. It doesn't matter if you initiate the changes or not. Once something has been observed and duly noted, changes start happening. These observations and changes are not necessarily about things we are unhappy about in our sex lives. We can observe things we are very happy with and these will change too.

I need more ...
'sex as I get older'

Time changes everything. Remember the thoughts you had about sex before you actually experienced it, or how you thought about sex a year, two years or a decade ago? Your thoughts have changed and probably the way you have sex has changed, even if you haven't attempted consciously to change anything. It just happens. Our feelings change as time passes, in the same way as our understanding of another person grows.

Everything – every thought, every action – has its time, its moment, and this time, this moment will pass. There is nothing we can do to stop it and it's not always painful or sad when something that has had its moment moves on. Sometimes it's absolutely wonderful. The level of pain we feel in a situation of ending something depends on the capacity we have to accept and recognise the necessity of the ending. The ending of a treasured relationship will be more painful than the ending of a bad phase within a relationship. It's all down to context.

However, using your will and making yourself move from a place or situation where you feel stuck gives you some degree of control over how you want changes made. You can identify any transformations that are needed and change them in any way you want. They were going to change, anyway, so why not nudge the changes in your choice of direction?

I need more ...
'freedom from the media, who always seem to be telling us how to do it'

When we wait for things to change or postpone taking action, then we are abdicating our responsibilities and handing over control to fate, which can also be a good thing because occasionally it is best to do nothing.

Let's return for a moment to Schrödinger's poor little cat in the box. You have addressed the situation, opened the box and seen the animal sleeping inside. What do you do? Do you give it a little poke and see if it wakes up? Do you take it to the animal-rescue hospital and let someone else deal with it? Do you get on the phone and tell someone about it? Do you put it in a sack and drown the thing? Do you walk away or leave making a decision about it until tomorrow?

It doesn't really matter. It's not a real cat: it's a theoretical postulation. A relationship is a living thing – it evolves and changes. Sex is real – we can see it and feel it and experience it. If we can change the fate of a theoretical cat simply by thinking and talking about it, think what we can do if we put our mind to things we care about, to things that matter to us, things that will make a difference to us as sexual beings.

I need more ...
'security and allowance for mistakes'

Get out of your bottle, Genie, it's time to start that wish thing happening.

The best time for sex is …
'when you're getting paid a lot of money'

The best time for sex is …
'midafternoon spontaneously'

I am …
'happy, attractive and deserve someone who tells me so'

I am …
'sexy and confident and feel good about my body'

'I … love sex, but *… sometimes it's hard to get it right'*

I want to feel …
'desired'

I'm too …
'conscious of my body'

I want …
'to continue having a good sex life for a long time'

I want to feel …
'loved and needed and have a bit of security in my life'

When I feel sexy, I …
'ignore it!'

What does sex do for you?
'It makes me feel more womanly. I work in a male-dominated workplace. I do quite a lot of physical labour. But sex always makes me feel one hundred per cent woman.'

15

Creating the Right Recipes

Sex isn't only about the physical act: it involves a whole host of feelings, judgements, preconceptions, values, beliefs, stories, lies, power, dominance, submission, eroticism, expectation and anticipation. That's just the thought processes around sex. The physical side of sex is as complex and varied as what goes on in our minds, so the widely touted concept of sex as 'what grown-ups do in bed together' isn't by any means the whole picture. It's more than that, much more, and it's also less than that.

Let's put aside the physical nature of sex for a moment. What I'm really interested in exploring is what goes on in our heads and in our minds regarding sex.

Allow me to use a little cookery metaphor here. When we want to eat, we each take ingredients and serve them up to satisfy ourselves – but we've got to have some idea of what we're hungry for. If we want meat and two veg, there's no point in whipping up masses of fresh cream and adding strawberries. We will have something to eat but not what we wanted. If we want to bake cupcakes, we'd better make sure we've got some of those little paper

I want to feel ...
'sexy and confident'

things to put them in and plenty of icing and silver balls for decoration. If we're ravenously hungry, anything will do, raw, straight out of the tin, standing up – we'll even pinch someone else's food.

Part of the joy of cooking and eating is that sense of curiosity and experimentation. However, if the ingredients are all wrong and the oven isn't at the right temperature, we're not going to end up with what we thought we were going to get. This doesn't necessarily mean that it will be inedible or horrible – sometimes the most spectacular culinary cockups are surprisingly tasty and enjoyable. Don't just look at it and go 'Yuk!' Close your eyes and taste it.

> **I want to feel ...**
> *'like the centre of the universe'*

Being open-minded and able to improvise is great when it comes to sex, just as it is with cooking. The thing about cooking is that, if you have an idea of what you want, it makes it easier to produce. Have you ever had one of those days when you fancy something to eat but don't know quite what it is you want? You prowl round the kitchen, nibbling things, but nothing really hits the spot. Cooking and eating is more than simply preparing and then putting food in your mouth and swallowing: it's a personal thing, a social thing, a lifestyle thing. It can give us pleasure, it can be painful and, like sex, it's a question of balance.

Sex is a balancing act of fulfilling our wants, needs and desires, and, at the same time, it is being aware of and sensitive to the wants, needs and desires of anyone else involved. Sometimes nobody else is involved, but you always are. These wants, needs and desires can be a hotchpotch of volatile factors that need careful handling to produce the desired results.

What do you want?

- Do you want to read a dirty book?

- Do you want to sneak off for a quickie right now?

- Do you want to be left alone?

- Do you want to roll naked in the morning dew and cover your skin with rose petals?

If there's only you involved, it's easy. You know exactly what you need to be satisfied at any given moment, but to relate to others you need to tell them what you want, otherwise how can they possibly know? Telling someone what you want isn't simply a case of saying 'I want this' and getting it. I wish it were, since life would be so easy, wouldn't it? Letting someone know what you want is about communicating with them.

I want to feel ...
'good about myself'

Communicating is more than speaking. We can *show* them what we want. We can set up little patterns, little anchoring devices, so that, when we give them that look, wear those clothes or move in a certain way, they are in no doubt as to our intentions.

We can drop hints, but they aren't always noticed. Even though we may consider ourselves sexually liberated, it can sometimes take a lot of inhibition-shedding to express exactly what it is we want. No matter how shy we are, bear this in mind: partners love to find out what we want.

If you want to explore new recipes in the sexual kitchen, the best way is to know what you want, what your partner wants and what strategies you are willing to explore to satisfy those wants.

If your desires involve another person, it is important that they are at least willing to cooperate and that you give them all the right signals. As I've said before, if you want meat and two veg, there's no point in whipping up a load of fresh cream. It's fun discovering ways to signal your intentions. If you want a lovey-dovey evening, put the whips and chains away, light a few candles and have some gentle music playing in the background. If you want to be a sex tart, get out your sexy clothes, wiggle your bottom and lay off the thermal underwear.

I want to feel ...
'loved, honoured and expressive'

If you are worried about reactions to the introduction of new ideas, sneak them in bit by bit. Coordinating effort is all about making sure everything heads in the same direction and finding the best way of getting the results you want.

Here's another thought. We can change the way our bodies look by changing what we eat and we can change the way we think of sex by changing our thoughts. We get what we focus on because that's one of the unwritten laws of the universe. Focusing on the wonderful, positive things that sex as a concept can bring will make us more open to the wonderful positive things that the physical act can give us.

You *can* have your cake and eat it. The best thing about doing so is sharing your cake if you feel like it. I don't know about you but I've never shared a cake with anyone who's offered me a lovely big slice of anxiety cake, filled with self-hatred and topped with a sprinkling of neurosis. Have your cake and eat it, but make sure it tastes good.

If your thoughts about sex were a cake, how would it taste? Just for fun, write down your list of ingredients and prepare your own recipe.

Does love play a part?
I guess, inextricably for me love plays a part at the moment. Not in the sense that it is all romantic, but in the sense that whatever I do sexually with another person is with a person I love (excluding fantasies).'

'**I** … *enjoy* **sex, but** … *for long-term relationships you need a lot more – respect and a sense of humour'*

'**I** … *don't have much* **sex, but** … *I don't feel that diminishes my sexuality'*

'**I** … *want* **sex, but** … *no one will shag me'*

I want to feel …
'wanted'

I want to feel …
'special like the only person in the world'

I know …
'how to give great blow jobs'

When I feel sexy, I …
'want to have sex with someone I fancy'

I wish for …
'time for the things I do'

I wish for …
'sex – we are several thousand miles apart and only spend a few days a month together. Regular sex, rather than a monthly marathon!'

16

The Devil Made Me Do It

The desire for the physical nature of sex can sometimes overrule everything else that is sex. Similarly, avoidance of the physical nature of sex can sometimes overrule everything else that sex encapsulates. Sex is more than a hot sweaty coming together of bodies; it's more than a half-baked fumble – and it's also so much less. Sex can be a thought, a gesture, wrapped up in the eroticism of an image, a lick of the lips, a curl of hair or an air of anticipation.

So what is this fascination that sex holds for us? Wars have been fought over it and governments overturned; it can ruin lives and it can create life. Businesses have been built on it; marriages can be made or broken by it; and every religion has its say on the subject.

What is it all about, this fear and fascination of raw, animalistic, uncivilised sexual impulses? What is the hold that sex has on us? We don't all fear sex. Some of us love it, not purely for the physical feelings we get from it but also because our sexuality is a manifestation of who we are. Things that we fear, loathe and despise in ourselves can reveal themselves through our sexuality. If we hold feelings of

When I feel sexy, I …
'ravish my partner'

shame about our bodies and sexual impulses, we can feel dirty and wicked, ugly and inferior, scared and ashamed of our fantasies and sexual feelings.

If we can learn to recognise our blocks and inhibitions and confront what we each consider to be our basest, most shameful aspects; we can free ourselves to release the creative power that is stifled by panic and self-disgust.

Make no bones about it – sexual creative power can be a magnificent thing. Do you have sexual fantasies? What a stupid question! It's like asking, 'Do you breathe out after you breathe in?' We all have sexual fantasies, each and every one of us, but some of us would never admit to it. That is fine because the wonderful thing about fantasies is that they are primarily for the pleasure of their creator. No one else need ever know what's causing you to smile and lick your lips.

> **When I feel sexy, I ...**
> *'flirt'*

For as long as I can remember, I have created sexual fantasies for my own amusement. Sometimes they linger for weeks while I elaborate on them, switching perspectives, changing people and places, getting them just right. Other times they last as long as it takes the stranger in the street to walk by ...

The delicious thing about fantasies is that nobody else need ever know. You can create your own secret, private world where anything is possible and there are no restrictions, judgements or taboos. You can indulge yourself anywhere.

Fantasies are a useful vehicle for us to peer into our own darkness, not only to look into the shadows but to embrace those shady corners of our imagination, or at least shed some light there. In a strange way, fantasies are a way of releasing ourselves from any restrictions and moral decisions we have imposed on ourselves in the real world, a way of mentally throwing off our shackles and overcoming obstacles that we have created for ourselves.

I'm sure I'm not alone in this, but I fantasise about all kinds of life's worst-case scenarios and how I would cope in certain situations. They are not always rude sexy ones: sometimes mundane, ordinary scenarios that can be elaborated upon. It's my way of exorcising those 'what would happen if …?' demons.

I fantasise about incredibly wonderful things happening in my life and what it would mean to me, how it would change me. I fantasise about being a bestselling author and appearing on chat shows, or about what kind of little old lady I will be. I fantasise about cooking the perfect meal, having a tidy house, burning all my old clothes and going out and buying a completely new wardrobe.

Fantasies allow us to try on for size our reactions if we were attacked, won the lottery, woke up and the house was on fire, were offered a golden opportunity, made something different happen in our life, sold millions of books, had a chance encounter with a movie star, started taking up skateboarding aged ninety or whatever we care to explore in our imagination.

> **When I feel sexy, I …**
> *'have a nice shower and bath, pamper myself and smell nice'*

I'm not suggesting that we abandon the real world and escape into our fantasy world where we can be in complete control and be our own superheroes. Our internal world of fantasy is a safe place to try out ideas, to rehearse, explore things that we know are probably never going to happen but we'd like to experience anyway in a safe environment, a place where we can change the scene, the cast and the viewpoint at any time. We can replay scenes, getting them exactly right; we can drop in what-if wildcards.

Sexual fantasies can be a way of escaping from a humdrum existence but they are also a wonderful way of adding to real life in all its glory.

So what do you fantasise about, sexually? I had a rather heated debate with a male colleague who thought he knew and understood women's fantasies. He had read Nancy Friday and considered himself to be an expert. However, I don't think he had ever spoken to a woman about her sexual fantasies and had a somewhat strange idea of women's inner thoughts. I wrote down a fantasy for him and he was rather taken aback at the rawness, the explicitness and the language. Perhaps it frightened him, I don't know – and I don't care. I didn't want to sleep with the guy. I merely wanted to enlighten him. The thing is, when it's your fantasy, you can do things, say things and be things that you might never consider acting out. How good is that?

> **When I feel sexy, I ...**
> *'probably blush'*

Fantasy is a great way of keeping the love juices flowing and I know I don't need to say it, but it is a splendid aid to orgasm, either on your own or with a partner. It can take you away from pain and lead you towards ecstasy but it isn't a replacement for real life. It's a way of adding to it.

Let's try out a few of those what-if sexual-fantasy scenarios. I'll start you off and the rest is up to you.

- What if … it was 1901, Buenos Aires, and you were the star turn in a high-class brothel? What is your speciality act?

- What if … you were naked on a bed in a hotel room and a stranger walked in?

- What if … you were the keeper of a sex stud farm and you could choose any of the studs and they would be more than happy to take orders from you? What would you order them to do to you?

- What if … a mysterious woman made a pass at you?

When I feel sexy, I …
'give my partner the shock of his life'

In the world of sexual fantasy, you are in charge of the results. I could give those scenarios to a hundred people and, if I could get them to tell me, there would be a hundred different responses to each. None of them would be wrong, some may be shocking, some may be tame, it doesn't matter. What matters is that it is your sexual fantasy, you guide the action and no one need ever know.

Start with 'What if …' and write down whatever pops into your head. Every now and then you may think, I can't possibly write that. Go ahead, write it – you may be amazed at where your fantasy world can take you. If you don't want anyone else to read them, keep them stashed away or throw them out afterwards. It's up to you. If nobody sees it, nobody can judge you. You don't even have to write it down – just sit and treat yourself to a quiet fantasy moment in your mind.

Giving ourselves the freedom to indulge in a little sexual fantasy doesn't automatically mean that we have turned to the 'dark side'. It's simply a device we have for doing things differently, freeing ourselves from our habitual ways and stereotypical reactions to situations.

Here's a liberating thought. The person we become in our sexual fantasy world doesn't have to be someone or something we aspire to. We don't need to have 'motivational' sexual fantasies. In today's world, we are bombarded with encouraging exhortations: 'Be high achieving! Reach for the stars! Aspire to better yourself! Be a modern superwoman! Have fulfilling meaningful sex! Motivate yourself to be the best you can be! Strive and smile!'

Sometimes I get sick of it all and I want to be a sleazy no-hoper. I can be that in my sexual fantasy world.

The world of sexual fantasy is a safe arena in which you can take your rule book and throw it out of the window. You can do or be anything you like, anywhere you like, with whatever or whomsoever you please, for as long as you like. Fantasy can be a lovely way of letting off some sexual steam, trying on ideas for size or whiling away a boring journey, lecture or meeting. But don't get so wrapped up in your fantasy world that you forget to engage with the real world.

When I feel sexy, I …
'wonder if anyone notices'

'I love **sex, but** … *it could be better – there's always something you think could be different, could be better*'

When I feel sexy, I … *'get wet'*

Does love play a part? *'Yes, love is essential to me, but not to all women'*

I know … *'we all search for love'*

I know … *'that there's room for improvement on my behalf'*

What do you believe about sex? *'I believe that, however dirty or risqué you think you are, there is always someone who has done something dirtier or more kinky (I used to work in a clinic).'*

What do you want from sex? *'Satisfying'*

Does love play a part? *'Yes, for me love always plays a part – it's not worth it otherwise – that mind connection'*

What do you believe about sex ? *'I believe that sex is powerful. Everyone lies about sex – I don't like talking about it with my mum but am incredibly graphic with my mates. Sex can mean control.'*

17

The Tower

We all want to avoid the worst possible scenarios, but what are they?

Relationships crumbling – that could be a worst-case scenario. It's not always the whole thing that crumbles: very often it can be a *part* of a relationship that falls to pieces. The relationship can be rock steady but the sex is flat and stale or the sex is wonderful but the relationship is failing fast. A sexual worst-case scenario can be anything that threatens to destroy or disrupt something that is important or dear to you.

We each build our towers of perfection, which can represent anything – protective towers that we build around ourselves to keep us safe, or towers we build to keep the world out. I'm not talking about real towers, by the way. I'm talking about the images we construct in our minds when we tell ourselves, 'That's the way it is, that's the way it must be, that's how I want it to be.'

> **I know** ...
> *'what he likes, he knows what I like'*

We then reinforce the way we want things by building a mental tower around the image, the thought or the ideal. Then we do everything we can to keep it that way. I'm not talking only about positive things.

We can build towers for ourselves that support negative views: for example, 'Every man I've ever known has been a selfish bastard'; 'Nobody will ever find me attractive'; or 'Nice people don't make noises in bed.'

They may sound like strange foundations for building towers but we have all built them and there are people who are constructing them right now. Maybe you are one of them.

We can build a tower for our lovers. 'This is what you are,' we say as we build their tower. 'This is how I see you; this is how easy or difficult I will make it for us to communicate. I will make these walls thick and strong because I don't want anyone else getting close.'

We build towers around our thoughts about sex, which some of us have kept locked for years. 'Don't go in there, there's a monster. Do anything you like but don't open that particular door.'

I know ...

'the longer I stay with a partner, the more I can please them'

We construct mental images of how we want to see the world and how we want the world to see us, and these towers serve to protect us and keep us safe within our comfort zones.

A tower is a symbol of safety, but what happens when it has been built in the wrong place, with the wrong materials? It could be the most beautiful, intricate, award-winning tower that makes people gasp with admiration, but, if it has been built on a rocky foundation, it is not so safe and indestructible after all.

When something comes along to challenge that belief and shake the very foundations of the tower, we can reinforce the walls and make them that bit thicker: for example, by finding proof that this man

who appears wonderful and lovely is in fact a
selfish bastard just like all the others, or by
not noticing people who are attracted to us.

When we find a man who isn't a selfish
bastard, or find someone who is attracted
to us, or we are noisy in bed and our lover
still thinks we are a nice person, what
happens to that tower of belief? It comes
tumbling down.

I know ...
*'I've put on weight and I've
got grey hair and he still
fancies me'*

If we've spent years building and maintaining the tower, it can be a
huge shock or an enormous relief when we stand by and finally
watch it topple. It is possible to place too much trust in thick
protective walls. It's a weird equation but the thicker the walls, the
narrower the view of the world.

The most elaborate towers we possess are often the ones we construct about sex. These represent the belief structures of our inner
and outer worlds, which we build for ourselves as defences against
life. Not only that, we can also use them as disguise, to hide our less
agreeable sides or dark secrets from others.

We can build a tower that presents the socially acceptable face to
hide the beast within. Yes, lock that scary part of ourselves away in a
tower so we never have to confront the outside world. That way only
the 'nice' us ever gets to see the light of day. Sooner or later our 'dark'
side will waste away and die, or get so angry at being locked away
and ignored, that it will burst through those walls to proclaim its
existence. The 'dark' side that some of us keep locked away isn't
always bad. It could simply be a side that wants hot dirty sex rather
than be made love to, or that wants experimentation rather than

routine, wants to grow old with one partner rather than try to keep young with many partners. Or vice versa.

Do we need these towers? Hell, yes. They're not only devices for protection and disguise but they allow us to know where we draw the line on any issue. For example, the office hunk sidles up and whispers in your ear, 'Want to sneak away with me for a dirty weekend? Go on, tell the husband it's work-related – no one will ever know.'

'I'd love to but hang on, let me check my tower. Actually, I'm a nice girl, I get plenty of sex at home, my family love me, I love them and, much as I'd like a frivolous fling with you, I don't want to jeopardise my beautiful tower.'

Towers that support us and protect us in a positive way are ultimately what we are trying to build. When they are built with things that constrain us or are held together with lies and deception, sooner or later cracks begin to show. Maybe not for a long time but when pressure is put on a weak construction, what happens? When something can no longer remain within its confines, either we can patch up the tower and hope it holds or watch it crumble and let it go.

I know ...
'how to enjoy myself'

For example, if two people have built up a relationship and it's built on rocky ground, sooner or later it will collapse. They either have to jump and start anew or stay and be destroyed. There are only two reasons why towers or relationships crumble: bad architecture and when they are built for all the wrong reasons.

Architecture is all about good, solid foundations, using the right materials with economy and style. It is also concerned with building

something in the right place, in order that it can
be used and enjoyed. Bad architecture demon-
strates a lack of awareness of what makes the
outside world tick, what has caused the
tower to be there in the first place and what
inspires and is valued by the owner of that
tower.

> **I know** ...
> *'that my partner also
> wishes I was a hot babe'*

The second reason they crumble is if they are built for all the wrong
reasons. Have you ever built a tower for somebody else and expected them to live in it? Or perhaps someone designed yours and you
tried to follow their instructions on how to build that tower.
Somehow it never really felt comfortable. If you've tried to construct
a tower that will satisfy everyone you may end up pleasing nobody,
least of all yourself.

Irrespective of whether you build your own towers or allow people
to build them for you, your personal towers represent your self-
image. Your self-image is your own conception of the person you are,
that product of past experiences, of good times, bad times, success-
es, humiliations, influences and rebellions. All these experiences
combine to build up a picture of yourself that you believe to be true.
We believe that we have those thoughts, habits and abilities. We *do*
actually have those thoughts, habits and abilities. They aren't made
up, we aren't lying to ourselves, but we have them only because we
gave them to ourselves and provided ourselves with the materials to
build them.

Imagine building a sexual self-image tower without using grudges
and feelings of resentment towards others. Imagine that it had no
sense of blame, that there were no foundations built on pain,

mistakes or embarrassment. Imagine a sexual self-image tower that allowed you to see yourself only at your best, allowed you to keep up with yourself at your own pace. Imagine the sign over the door of this tower, which reads, 'Live your own life and don't be too concerned with how others live theirs.'

Build your towers and make sure you build them as well as you can, with the best possible foundations, and turn them into nice towers. You don't have to make them dark, foreboding places. Your tower may be a place of sanctuary, of self-definition, a mirror to your soul, but it doesn't have to be an ivory tower or a prison, and neither should it be a museum containing people or things to blame for what's gone wrong in your life.

Do a bit of a redevelopment. If any of your towers keep you in a rut or separate you from any activity, situation or people that you want to be involved with, knock that tower down or at least rebuild or redecorate it to allow yourself some flexibility.

Once we free ourselves from narrow viewpoints, we can find that our horizons widen and our perspective on life changes. When we build our towers on firm foundations, every moment can be a preparation for a positive future rather than another nail in the door.

> **I know …**
> *'me and my partner should talk about sex more'*

Open up that barrier and let the future in. There's a glorious world of possibilities out there waiting for you.

What do you believe about sex?

I believe that sex can be very satisfying and enjoyable for all parties when they each know what satisfies the other'

'I feel sexy when others find me attractive'

When I feel sexy, I ...

'think fantasy things, feel sultry'

I need more ...

'reassurance that I am not a sex object, that my feelings also count, that I can express my feelings as well'

I want to feel ...

'horny, sexy and like I'm turning someone else on'

I know ...

'a few things about sex, but not a lot – how to switch myself off when I need to'

I am ...

'not getting it as often as I did when I was first married or before my little angel arrived into my life'

I need more ...

'encouragement'

'I ... *love* **sex, but ...**

want every time to carry an intensity'

18

Starlight, Starbright

However wonderful, magical, perfect or fulfilling our lives, or indeed our sex lives, may be, we can always find something more to wish for. Generally speaking, the higher up the happiness ladder we are, the more specific our wishes will be.

Let's indulge in a little make-believe and imagine that maybe, for whatever reason, you are not having sex at all and you want a bit of carnality in your life. The scene we'll set is this: you are hungry for sex and anything will satiate you. What do you wish for? Sex. Absolute bottom line. Sex. That's what you're not getting and that's what you want.

Now, let's say that you are getting sex but it is not satisfying you the way you want it to, what do you wish for now? *Satisfying* sex.

I wish for ...
'happiness'

Moving on to the next imaginary level, maybe you are having satisfying sex but it is always with a different lover and you want to experience satisfying sex with one lover over a period of time. What do you wish for? A long-lasting satisfying sexual relationship, perhaps?

156

You get that but you can't stand the person who makes your body quiver with pleasure. What do you wish for now? To have positive feelings about your lover? To find someone who can give you all the pleasure that your present lover gives you but they must be someone that you fancy? Who knows? The impor-

I wish for ...
'sex!'

tant thing to learn here is that we all wish for things, sometimes greater things than we already have, sometimes more detailed and specific things. We want more of what we already have, or less. We wish for things to be different, or for them to stay exactly the same.

That's nothing new: mankind has always been this way.

The amazing thing is that there is no limit to the number of wishes we can have. Whatever you may have been told in the past, the wishing star won't wear out. You can wish for whatever you want and, what's more, wishes can come true.

I feel like the fairy godmother who waves her wand and says, 'You can have as many wishes as you like. But ...'

Sorry, there always has to be a 'but'. It's known as the 'conditional clause'. You can wish for whatever you want, *but*: be home by the stroke of midnight; give me your firstborn; kiss the frog; tell nobody.

I'm here to help you reclaim that fairy-tale optimism. You can wish for whatever you want, wishes can come true and there's no limit to the amount of wishes you can have ... wait for it ... here it comes ... the conditional clause ... *but* ... But the nearer your wishes are to where you are at that moment in time, the more likely it is that they will come true.

If you lock yourself away in a windowless room and make a wish to meet people, your wish has much less chance of manifesting than if you walked from your windowless room, picked up the phone, rang a few friends and told them about your wish. Wishes come true, *but* you've got to give them a helping hand and meet them halfway at least.

Let's bring all this back to sex, after all, that's what this book is about. One fundamental thing you need to know about sex is that you *can* have whatever you wish for. I know that some of you are sitting here thinking, 'That's so not true: I wish for things and they never come true.' And you're absolutely right. It's good to question things that are in direct contradiction to what you've experienced. In fact, it's a fundamental, essential thing. What's the alternative – accepting everything, or refusing to accept anything? Either way, you'll be selling yourself short.

I wish for ...
'love'

Never, never believe everything you are told. Once you start believing everything, your life becomes a series of absolutes that must be upheld at all costs, or they crumble and you are left with nothing. Once you begin questioning things – 'Why does it have to be this way?'; 'What would happen if …?'; 'How do you know this?'; 'Is there any way it could be the opposite of this?' – then everything becomes tangible, changeable and you are put in control. Absolutes are unquestionable and unchanging; tangibles are flexible and changeable.

When we live our lives as a series of absolutes, making wishes come true becomes very difficult. Think of something in your life that you consider to be an absolute. For example:

- 'We only have sex on Friday night'

- 'I can't find a partner'

- 'Everything is wonderful'

- 'I don't know how to turn my partner on'

- 'I am a sex addict, I can't control myself'

- 'I am not going to change'

What would you need to do to change these absolutes into possible realities? Sometimes one word is all that's needed to change a perspective. That magic word so often used by the fairy godmothers – 'but' – can be used to soften an absolute, magically turning it into a tangible and opening it up to possibility thinking:

> **I wish for** ...
> *'good oral sex (not lollipop licking) and more gentle lovemaking'*

- 'We only have sex on Friday night, but ...'

- 'I can't find a partner, but ...'

- 'I don't know how to turn my partner on, but ...'

Here are a few other magic words that can help soften those absolutes or melt those granite beliefs so we can get closer to making wishes come true:

Put those absolutes in the past tense. For example:

- 'We only *had* sex on Friday night ...'

- '*I couldn't* find a partner ...'

- 'I *didn't* know how to turn my partner on ...'

If something is put into the past tense, it weakens. To make the magic work and make those wishes come true, strike while the iron is hot, when the absolute is weakening.

Let's use one of those absolutes as an example of wish making and how to make them come true.

- 'I don't know how to turn my partner on.'

So what is your wish?

- 'I wish I knew how to turn my partner on.'

I wish for ...
'*time, patience and a fucking man*'

In what way will the fact that you didn't know how to turn your partner on, and you are now aware of this, help you to know how to rectify the situation? Does it open your mind to the possibility of experimentation? Think about this for as long as you need and make your wish come true. Let the magic happen.

It's only words, but already I can feel that absolute weakening. Let's play with another absolute:

- 'I am a sex addict – I can't control myself.'

And your wish is ...?

- 'I wish I could exercise some control over my sexual appetite.'

So, when your wish is granted, you will feel in control of your sexual appetite? You will feel in control now that your wish has come true? Is that right?

Now that you think about your wish, in what way does the addiction you had to sex actually mean that you can now be in control of your sexual urges?

Think about this. Wishes are only words, and the magic that makes wishes come true is very often only words. When we make wishes, it helps to consider where we are now in relation to where we want to be in order to have those wishes materialise. Another point often overlooked by unsuccessful wish makers is this: 'If the wish were to come true, what would it give me?'

In order to move wishes into the real world, we need to ask ourselves, 'What would this wish give me if it were to come true?' and 'What is the purpose of wishing for this?'

Wish for whatever you want and then ask yourself, 'What will this wish give me?'

We find it easy to wish for things in the material world – a new car, a team of experienced interior designers to redesign your house, a health guru for your body, a fashion expert to revamp your wardrobe. We wish for enough money, more time, more space and better relationships – but what do you wish for sexually? Is it something physical – a lover with an enormous penis, a waterbed, an impressive array of sex toys, hot sex with that movie star?

I wish for ...
'confidence, sometimes'

Or is it more of a state of mind? Happiness, feeling loved, finding a soul mate, something to make the pain go away? Feeling wanted? Fun?

Wishes for physical things are very different from wishes for feelings or states of mind. Or are they? It is obvious when you have been granted your physical wish – if, for example, you get a lover with a huge penis, you somehow just know. Feelings are a little more difficult to pin down, yet they are at the core of wish making. Feelings are the part that makes the magic happen, makes the wish come true. Feelings are what every wish boils down to.

I wish for ...
'excitement'

By way of demonstration, let me select something at random from my sex wish list: 'I wish I had a water bed.' Now I ask myself some questions about what my waterbed will give me:

- 'What is the purpose of having a waterbed?' *It will give me something exciting to have sex on.*

- 'And what is the purpose of having something exciting to have sex on?' *It will make me feel sexy and adventurous.*

- 'And what is the purpose of feeling sexy and adventurous?' *I will feel good about myself and have fun with my partner.*

- 'And what is the purpose of feeling good about myself and having fun with my partner?' *I will feel happy and sexy.*

So, the ultimate aim has nothing to do with a waterbed: it is all about the wish to be feeling something.

Wishes are all about the manifestation of feelings.
Try it yourself: take anything you wish for sexually and subject it to the 'What is the purpose of …?' questioning pattern. You can also
double-check with 'What will … give you or
lead to?'

I wish for …
'condoms'

See how it all boils down to feelings?

So, here's how you can make wishes come true: cut out all the
rubbish and head straight for the feeling. Let's say that the ultimate
feeling you are after sexually is happiness. It doesn't have to be
happiness: it could be a feeling of belonging, of bliss, of peace, of
revenge or rebellion. Find the feeling you are after behind the wish.
Then, when you've distilled the wish and found the feeling you
are after, the next step is to consider, 'What else will give me that
feeling?'

There is no guarantee that having sex with Mr Fabulous Filmstar,
having a waterbed or even experiencing a magnificent penis will
bring happiness. Even having sex on a waterbed with Mr Fabulous
Filmstar and discovering he's hugely well endowed is no guarantee
of a specific feeling. We can wrap a feeling around anything but we
can't guarantee that something will automatically give us a particular
feeling.

So, when making wishes, be careful what you wish for. 'When you
wish upon a star …' Isn't that how the old song goes? But what is a
star? It is a bright light surrounded by darkness, a clearly defined
source of energy – and that is exactly what a wish is. Context makes
the wish come true and, because context is everything, you can
create whatever you want around that energy source.

If you have taken the time to wish for something and identified that something as being attainable, you have to move towards it and touch it. Don't waste time and effort by simply wishing on a star: move towards those wishes. Wishes are powerful forces, but only if you act on them.

I once wished I could write this book. My wish has come true, but it didn't just appear by magic on my trusty laptop. I had to sit at my desk and type.

> **I wish for ...**
> *'encouragement'*

When we make wishes and move towards them, wishes are always fulfilled, not always as we expect but even the unexpected can be a good result. The good thing about wishes is that they give us hope, give us a goal to aim for and allow us to widen our horizons.

We may not reach our wish at all but, in making the effort, we offer ourselves hope and inspiration.

Hope can transcend anything life offers. And what is a wish? It's a hope with balls, a hope with energy, a hope with magic.

Wishes are wonderful things but, when we live our lives continually in a state of 'I wish ...', we begin to lose sight of the here and now.

The best time for
sex is …
'straight after a stressful day
at work'

I am …
'loving and insecure in certain
things, including career and love'

'I … love **sex, but** …
sometimes fail to give sex the
respect it deserves. And also I don't
respect myself sexually enough'

I need
more …
'time for sex'

I want to feel …
'relaxed, loved, needed and
wanted all in one go'

I'm too …
'fake sometimes – I let people
take advantage too much and
also don't tell people what I
really think enough'

When I feel
sexy, I …
'am probably
ovulating'

I know…
'that I am a worthwhile person whether I am
having sex or not!'

19

Howling at the Moon

Sex is just sex. Is that all it is, just sex? I don't think so, and I'm sure that you don't, either. Sex is as complex and as multifaceted as we are. It all depends on the context. The context defines what sex is at any given moment. The context can change the simple abstract notion of something called sex into a thought, a celebration, an intention, a fuck, instant gratification, making love, creating life, a violation, a way of making money, something right, something wrong, a beautiful, meaningful experience, something you used to do or a million other things.

Context is everything. It is the difference between the story and the plot. The story is the objective point of view. Sex and the plot is the context, the subjective point of view, the thing that gives it meaning. Let me illustrate this idea of context and plot.

I'm too …
'irritable – when he bugs me, I don't feel like sex at all'

Here's the story. Two people are having sex. That's the objective story. Picture in your mind the story of two people having sex. The picture you come up with. That's the plot, the context.

So how does that work? You pictured two people having sex, just as I asked you to do, so how can that be subjective? There is no context there. It's a thought of two people having sex. No plot, just sex.

But it isn't just sex, though, is it? The image you created in your mind was the plot, the context, your subjective interpretation of two people having sex. You had an infinite choice of how to picture two people having sex and you made your choice.

Perhaps the two people were at opposite ends of the world, talking each other to orgasm over the phone. Maybe they were teenagers furtively having sex, hoping they wouldn't wake the parents. Maybe only one was willing, maybe neither of them was. One or both of them were laughing, perhaps, or crying. Maybe this was the most tender, beautiful moment they had ever experienced or perhaps they were in front of a film crew and it was all part of a day's work. Same sex, different sex; same ages, different ages; ugly, beautiful, clothed, undressed – any could have appeared in your imagination. Maybe they were sitting at a table, having a meal that was called 'sex' on the menu.

I'm too …
'shy'

Stories are such simple things but the plots and the contexts we build around our stories can change everything. Even though two people can experience the same story, they each build their own plots around the story, personalise and own the new reworking. Most of the time we do this without realising. We forget the original story and get lost in the plot. Contrary to popular belief, sometimes it's good to lose the plot and take a look at the original story. That way we can see whether the plot we made for the story is working for us, whether it helps us, or whether it is useful.

For example, let's imagine you had a bad sexual experience some time ago (story = bad sexual experience in the past). You put it all into context, structuring your plot to read:

> I had a bad experience but I have learned from it. I cried but I got over it. As a result of that experience, I'm stronger and wiser and I won't let anyone try that shit with me again.

The plot would have a completely different feel to it had you chosen a different context for the same story:

> I had a bad experience and it's completely ruined my life. I keep repeating the same pattern and it happens again and again. I want everyone to know that I have been a victim, so that they will know how much I'm suffering.

See how it works? Same story – bad sexual experience in the past – but the different plots and contexts sow the seeds for different endings. Neither of the plots is true; they become true only at the minute you start to own them.

You write the plot and, if it isn't working for you, you can change it. Lose the plot. Or create a new one.

I'm too ...
'bothered about my figure'

In researching this book, I interviewed a working girl – a woman who has sex for money – and the plot worked for her because she could dissociate her feelings when she was working and claim them back again when she was with her partner. She enjoyed what she did, she was very good at it and she wasn't going to write the words 'victim' or 'pity me' into her plot.

I interviewed widows who had lost their husbands years ago. They had set out the plot as, 'I had wonderful sex with my husband and I don't need or want sex any more.'

I spoke to two middle-aged women who told me, amid gales of laughter, that they found sex to be too painful after having children but have since discovered the joys of hand jobs and blow jobs.

I spoke with an older man who told me that, in his youth, his main preoccupation with sex was to sow his seeds as far and wide as possible. As he got older, he changed his plot to search for 'the one'. After fifty-five years of being with 'the one', his plot had changed from discovering what turns each other on to being happy just being together.

Other women told me their plots. Some said they would love a more adventurous sex life but could never find the time; others deliberately made time to be alone with their partners. Some hadn't had or thought about sex in a while and it didn't bother them in the slightest. Some hadn't had sex in a while and it was as though their world were coming to an end. They were all writing their own plots.

I'm too ...
'busy'

I had sixteen questions that I asked when interviewing people for this book and those questions revealed many, many individual plots in people's lives. Some people write happy plots for themselves, some don't. If you are happy with the plot you write for yourself, that is a wonderful achievement. Nobody else can write one for you. They may try and they do try, don't they? How many times have you heard people telling you:

- 'You should be ....'

- 'This is the way it will be ...'

- 'You need to be stronger... weaker... more laid back... more careful ...'

I'm too ...
'needy'

We go along with their ideas of what our plot should be, because in some strange way it suits us. Perhaps it gives us something to rebel against or a reason to be a victim. We sometimes let others take over our plot because, let's face it, it makes for an easy life and saves arguments. It saves having to make our own decisions or – possibly because it makes them happy – we let them write the plot for us.

We write our own plots and when we take on board someone else's impositions or suggestions we *choose* to do this. We have unconsciously weighed up all the alternatives and gone for the easiest option, which can mean keeping the peace, keeping everyone happy, keeping our heads down or staying alive.

Most of the time, others want to get involved with your plot because they care about you, but care is a subjective thing, too. Too much caring can feel like being wrapped up in cotton wool and not being allowed to breathe. Or it can feel wonderful. It depends on the context. All is never what it seems because we each add our individual interpretations to any given story.

What is that story? This is a chaotic, confusing, unbounded world in which an individual plays only a small part. We exist within a universe of infinite possibilities and each and every one of us carries within him or her the potential to be magnificent. Then again, it depends on how you define magnificent, doesn't it?

It also depends on the point of view. Maybe you are out there, claiming your inherent right to magnificence, and to the observer you are nothing more than a prat. Or 'that woman who jogs'. Or 'the mousy one at the back of the class'.

You can't control where you will fit into anybody else's plot. You may feel as though you are the moon revolving around their sky but they may see you as a lump of grey rock that changes from day to day. You may feel like nothing more than a lonely lump of grey rock yourself but to somebody, somewhere, you are the eternally mysterious ever-changing moon, illuminating their dark sky. Don't laugh. It happens.

I'm too ...
'worried about my appearance and sexual abilities'

Inside each and every one of us is a wild creature who wants occasionally to be let out to howl at the moon.

Do you ever lose your plot? Do you ever abandon that carefully crafted and delicately honed interpretation of what you believe sex means to you? Do you ever look at things from a completely different point of view, change the perspective and rediscover the magnificent mysteries within?

Every now and then, abandon the old you and howl at the moon. Look at the script you are writing for yourself and see if it still fits. Like the moon and the scripts that suited us once, we change over time and things that once felt good and fitted us perfectly can start to feel tight or baggy. The wonderful thing is that sometimes, when we lose the plot, howl at the moon and take a long look at what sex means to us, we find that the plot we are creating really does suit us.

It seems that we spend so much time trying to unravel life's mysteries, when sometimes all we need to do is to get a new perspective and look at the bigger picture. An appreciation of life's simple pleasures is what drives most of us. The laws of nature are simple ones and sometimes the stories we create for ourselves get so complicated and confusing that it helps to stop and rise above it all in order to get a handle on what it was supposed to be about in the first place.

Sex can be one of life's simplest pleasures. It can also be completely and utterly dreadful, depending on how we write our scripts.

So, what angle should I be going for on this 'write my own life script and create my own context' thing?

Any angle you want.

I'm too ...
'fucking fed up of looking'

But ... How do I get others to support me in this? It's all right deciding on, for example, a joyful, blissful sex life but, if others won't support me in my objective, what do I do?

What do you want to do?

The best time for sex is …
'after a good night out and you're all full of energy'

'I … *like* sex, but …
sometimes find it to be a pain in the arse because it causes fights and arguments and I hate it when he wants it and I don't because it's on the back of my mind and I feel guilty for not giving it'

What do you believe about sex?
'It can be absolutely wonderful, but can be the worst possible experience in the wrong circumstances'

I know …
'that I can get plenty with just one man'

Does love play a part?
'It's nice when it does, but you can have different types of sex – from a fuck to a spiritual connection'

What do you want from sex?
'To be close and intimate with my partner and have an orgasm – or two'

When I feel sexy, I …
'feel good about myself'

I know…
'that my relationship is not perfect by any means, but I'm trying'

20

The Only Time We Have is Now

Sex is one of life's fundamentals, like breathing, like eating and drinking, like the need for warmth, light and sleep. We have to breathe but we do exercise some control over how much nourishment, warmth, light and sex we choose to experience. We all tolerate or enjoy different amounts of nourishment, warmth, light and sex.

When I'm hungry, I eat. I also eat when I'm not hungry, for many reasons. A lot of my social drinking has nothing to do with being thirsty. It has to do with pleasure, and pleasure is one of the guiding forces in my life. I'm not alone in admitting that pleasure is one of the things that shape my preferences and decisions.

When I feel sexy, I …
'want my partner to feel sexy and get just as much out of it'

There's this big pleasure principle that governs most of our fundamental needs. We move away from pain and towards pleasure. Some people move away from pleasure and towards pain unconsciously, and there's the often unack-nowledged issue of getting pleasure from pain, not necessarily in a sadomasochistic sense but for revenge, martyrdom or to prove a point.

There are many reasons why we have sex or why we do or don't entertain our feelings of sexuality, and very few of them have anything to do with what we were told in the school sex education classes, that the primary function of sex is reproduction. Sex, as a concept is there for us to create feelings about ourselves, irrespective of whether we are sworn to celibacy or whether we are the feistiest sex addict who ever walked on this earth.

When I feel sexy, I ...
'feel good'

So how do we get others to share these feelings with us? If we want sex to be an intimate act between two consenting people, how can we get the other person to feel as we do? The simple answer is: you can't. You can light all the candles you want, put on the sexiest music you can find, oil 'em and spoil 'em, but you can't *make* them feel how you want them to feel. Each and every one of us is a separate being and we come together in an intimate way through sex, but can't control what goes on in each other's mind.

In the right circumstances turning someone on is easy. There's an old saying: to turn a woman on, be tender, loving, attentive and willing to be her slave; to turn a man on, turn up naked and bring beer.

It's easy to turn someone on but you can't make someone feel the way you want them to feel. However, you can influence them. It's all to do with communication. Communication is all about getting what you want and giving someone what they need at the same time. It's about perception and projection – giving out what you receive, how you perceive things, what you are thinking at any given moment: 'They won't enjoy this'; 'They're bored'; 'I hate my body'; 'I'm the sexiest woman in the world'; 'This is amazing.' What you think is what you project onto the world.

You are the source of your passion. If you feel that your sex life is dull, then that is what you project and that is what you will get. If you use your inner state (the way you are feeling) to create outer realities, you can manifest anything, good or bad.

Have you ever done the 'act as if' thing with sex? It's a bit like faking it except that it allows us to intensify a feeling or emotion so much that it feels real. If you have never tried acting as if, have a go. You don't even have to let your lover in on the 'act as if': it can be all for your entertainment, if you want it to be.

What should I 'act as if'? Anything you want. Here are a few random examples. Next time you have sex, act as if you were both virgins, exploring each other for the first time, or act as if this were to be the last time you have sex before the end of the world. Act as if you were with the most magnificent lover in the world or act as if you had a pile of laundry that needs ironing and you really should be doing that rather than having sex. Act as if your lover were unimaginative and you were cold and frigid. It works both ways. Perception is projection.

> **When I feel sexy, I …**
> *'grab hold of his arse and get upstairs'*

As we near the end of this book, I want to concentrate on the good stuff that sex can bring.

If you have an abundant and joyful attitude or approach to sexuality in which you can find joy, happiness and release, then it becomes infectious and the world is your oyster.

It's time to celebrate what's good about your sex life, what's good about your sexuality. We do enough moaning about what's wrong and, if ever there was a prize for the person who had the worst sexual experience, we'd all be telling our stories and fighting each other for it. The tales I could tell … About when I was single … When I had three lovers on the go at once … When I went off sex completely … And yet with a different perspective, I could tell you wonderful things about my sex life … About when I was single … When I had three lovers on the go at once … When I went off sex completely …

But this book isn't about me. It's not particularly about sex, either. It's about unlocking the secrets of sensual desire, and thinking sexy. It's about ways of looking at ourselves and our expectations and being in charge of our own destiny. Let's face it, sex is a pretty central force in defining our destiny. Sex has shaped the futures of queens, kings, presidents, poets, artists, chip shop owners, teachers and lawyers, as well as you and me.

> **When I feel sexy, I …**
> *'must have sex, but if no one is about I will get my toys out'*

We all live our lives under the same sun and we all share that same potential ability to appreciate life's simple pleasures – and sex is one of those pleasures.

So what is so special about it? What makes it such a powerful force? Sex is not only about the physical and sexual. It is powerful because it can lead to ecstasy – and even without the ecstasy, sex can be an intense sensory experience.

So what exactly is ecstasy? Ecstasy is many things to many people, but in essence it is that feeling of being completely in the here and now and not giving a hoot at that moment about what the rest of the world is thinking or doing. That state of ecstasy is an extraordinary sense of feeling in which the mind becomes detached from sensible things and experiences enormous joy or enthusiasm.

Ecstasy can be experienced by anyone. It is a moment of unconditional love, of absolute perfection in that moment, of feeling filled with … with what? Here's a few states to whet your appetite: Joy; delight; elation; bliss; rapture; excitement; pleasure; seventh heaven; fulfilment; completion; realisation; abandonment.

However we frame them, they all sound like rather splendid states to experience, and they sound pretty much like how it feels to experience an orgasm. But sex isn't just about orgasms. I'm sure I'm not alone in being willing to sacrifice many things for that fleeting moment of magnificent orgasm. Whatever else is going on in your life, that short wave of rapture can bring a feeling of being right here, right now, totally in the moment. It can give you instant momentary bliss and, in that moment, allow you to let go of wanting.

When I feel sexy, I …
'am feeling confident about my body and how I look'

Isn't that what we are all looking for? If only life were that simple!

Is pleasure really such a driving force? It seems so. There have been scientific experiments to prove that beings will even forego food for pleasure to the point of starvation. Years ago, I heard about an experiment with rats, where the rats were trained to tap one button for food and one button for pleasure stimulation. A small electric current was sent to the 'pleasure centre' of the rat's brain. The scientists developed the experiment to train the rats so that they knew they could only press one button a day. They could have either food or pleasure stimulation. Guess what? The rats preferred pleasure. Some of the rats even starved themselves to death. But they died with smiles on their furry little faces.

Sex gives us pleasure. We don't always experience the pleasure in the same way – some of us tune into only the physical pleasure and some of us love the pleasure of anticipation. The pleasure of revenge, of martyrdom, of suffering – these all can be and are connected to sex. The pleasure of purity, the pleasure of conquest, the pleasure of familiarity, the pleasure of discovery. The pleasure of being intimate with someone we love. They're all there, linked to sex for us to enjoy.

What's to stop you feeling good about sex? You have everything there you need; it's all within reach if you start looking.

There's that often-experienced thought about how the grass is always greener on the other side, and it can stop us from experiencing joy in the here and now. How often have we told ourselves the following? 'The last one was good/bad, the next one will be perfect – but the present? It's not right at all – in fact it's awful.'

> **When I feel sexy, I …**
> *'have sex'*

Right now is the only time we have. What's happened before is over and gone. None of us can rely on tomorrow. Dreams and happiness start here, at this moment. If you missed that moment, don't worry, catch the next one – here it comes.

Don't try to feel good about sex with all its multifaceted trimmings. Trying to do something never gets it done. Just do it. Don't put it off until tomorrow. Why put all your faith in something that never arrives? Enjoying the thought of sex won't turn you into a raving sex maniac or a pervert. It will simply give you another tool to embrace your vitality and zest for life with all its joy and richness. Remember, it's infectious – perception is projection.

If you perceive sex to be a natural by-product of life around which you can build whatever rules you wish, then that is what you project onto the world and what others will experience from you. I'm not only talking about the physical act of sex. That's the tip of the iceberg. Sex, as a subject, is huge. Dive in and surprise yourself.

There's a whole world out there and we don't have to share sex with any of it if we don't want to, but, when we do choose to share, make sure to do that little ecology check.

When I feel sexy, I …
'ping my G-string!'

Sex is about many things but, fundamentally, it is about the ways of thinking and patterns of behaviour we set ourselves. Sex begins and ends with a thought and sometimes, just sometimes, there's something physical that goes on in the middle. Our job as individuals is to make sure that the thoughts we have about sex benefit us and those around us.

Postscript

We've Come a Long Way
(a Gentle Reminder)

Have you ever discovered something, learned something new, per-haps, or been reminded of something you already knew but had for-gotten? It feels good, doesn't it, having that feeling of 'I know that'?

Maybe now you are feeling that you know a lot more about sex than you realised. I wonder if you realise that you have learned or remem-bered a lot of things while reading this book and that some of those things had nothing whatsoever to do with the book. How good does that feel? Even if you feel that you've learned nothing, your uncon-scious will have been storing little nuggets of information along the way, just as it always does, and you'll remember them at exactly the right time because that's its job. Your inner mind has one function, and that's to do right by you. You may consciously forget everything you have read but, when the time comes, information or insights that are useful to you will pop into your consciousness and you won't even realise that it's happening.

Just for a moment, take your mind back to the time when you began reading this book and remember how, occasionally, you felt really good – when something made sense, made you laugh, made you aware of how much you already knew.

Within the pages you will have found revelations and self-discoveries softly unfurling.

We've been on a journey of discovery, you and I.

Do you remember how, at the beginning of the book, we learned about beginnings? How the beginning of anything, a thought, an awareness, a relationship, or even starting a book, is all about energy, curiosity and making room for the unexpected.

Do you remember reading about how to make sex magical and common sex myths in Chapter 2? There are sex myths by the cartload and you've probably created a few yourself or taken on board myths that others have created for you. I can think of a few others right now:

- 'You'll never get laid looking like that' – Ho, ho, ho, how wrong was that one?

- 'Once you have kids, you can kiss your sex life goodbye' – Oh yeah?

- 'Old people know nothing about sex' – old people know more about sex than anybody. They just keep quiet about the fact that they were doing it before half of us were born.

We explored the idea that you are the one who has the last word on how much you are going to enjoy something. We looked at how the awakening of senses, perceptions and ideas all begin in the mind. Our natural sense of curiosity, genuine responses and unbridled emotions are hidden deep down, under layers of conditioned feelings, patterns of behaviours and self-imposed imperatives.

Remember the breath anchor? Have you played with using it in different situations? Go on, have fun with it. Next time you are too tired to have sex, or in a job interview or sitting in the dentist's chair, or any situation where you would normally be filled with anxiety, try it out.

In Chapter 4, we looked at personal sexual abundance, ways of thinking, ways to look differently at things and ideas to open your mind even more and embrace possibility thinking, and anything is possible now, isn't it?

We discovered that there are no absolutes, we can set our own rules and we can change our rules as often as we want. We have the last and first word about where the power and influence lies in our sex lives, whether it's the power to say: 'I'm in a rut, it feels comfortable and I've no intention of changing anything, it suits me fine'; or, 'You're not getting anywhere near my knickers until you've finished tiling the bathroom like you promised.'

We celebrated and berated those infamous deadly sins: pride; envy; gluttony; lust; sloth; anger; greed and discovered how to find our individual personal sexual philosophy – the set of guidelines we give ourselves to determine how we react and respond to sex.

Do you remember the script the sexual eco-warrior within uses to filter and be aware of possible consequences?

- 'Am I OK with this? Are others OK with this? What are the positive and negative effects of this? What is this an example of? What is its purpose? What will I gain or lose? What won't happen? What will happen?'

Now that you have become aware of that sexual eco-warrior part of you, remember to tune into it now and then. It's always there, but usually talking so quietly that we choose not to listen.

We looked at how our feelings and emotions about sex are all motivated by three basic conflicts and desires. Sexual power, sexual satisfaction and sexual stability. They may well be the foundations for every sexual conflict or desire that we experience but we are the architects. Never forget that.

When it comes to sex, what do you now believe about yourself? What do you now believe you are capable of? What do you now believe about sex? What has changed within yourself after reading this book? Contrary to misconceptions, there's no such thing as good or bad change, only different perceptions of how change affects us. We looked at change within a relationship and looked at things that affect how we change, how our partner changes, the world changes, how a relationship, as an entity in itself, changes. Everything changes and nothing stays the same.

We've looked at how we manipulate our judgements in order to see the world in a way that suits us, we've discovered the pros and cons of sexual martyrdom and explored the idea of what we would wish for if we could start with a completely clean slate. It's been fun, hasn't it?

Do you remember reading about sex being a balancing act of fulfilling our wants, needs, desires and at the same time, being aware and sensitive to the wants, needs and desires of anyone else involved? And we explored the fear and fascination of raw, animalistic, uncivilised sexual impulses – fun, frolics and fantasies and what lies lurking in the deep recesses of our imaginations.

We looked at how and why we build protective towers around ourselves, how we attempt to build towers for others and why some towers are useful and others are simply a folly.

Remember how to make wishes come true? Cut out all the nonsense and look for the feeling you are after. Everything else is simply icing on the cake.

We revealed the difference between the story and the plots we create within them and discovered that we often forget what the original story was and get lost in the plot.

We've looked at the many reasons why we have sex, why we do or don't entertain our feelings of sexuality and about Right Now being the only time we have.

So, what more do you need to know? Need to know about sex positions? Experiment and discover what works for you. Want to know about contraception? Get out there and explore what style of contraception suits you. Want to know when the right time to have sex is? If it feels right for you and you've done the old eco check, any time is right.

Want to know how to really turn your lover on? Ask them. (Or turn up naked and bring beer). Get them to show you where and how they like to be touched. They'll tell you. All you need to do is ask.

If you are one of those people who like to read the last couple of chapters of a book first so that you can identify the hero, who did it, who is the baddie and what the book is about, I'll tell you right now. It's you. You're the star, you're the villain and you're the reason for the story. You're going to have to read the rest of the book to work out how you managed to arrive at centre stage.

During the last few months while I've been researching and writing this book, people I haven't seen for a while have asked me what I'm up to. When I tell them I'm writing a book about sex, they're interested, they want to know, they want to talk about sex. Sex as a subject is fascinating and draws us, like moths to a flame. We want to know, we like to know about sex.

We are all different, have our own lives and histories, our own particular needs and desires. This book will show you how to deal with where sex starts.

Take a moment, sit back, close your eyes and take in a slow, languorous, deep breath, hold it for a second or two and then blow the breath out, gently through your lips. Do it now. Remember how good it feels?

Close the book now and open up that most sensual of organs – your mind.